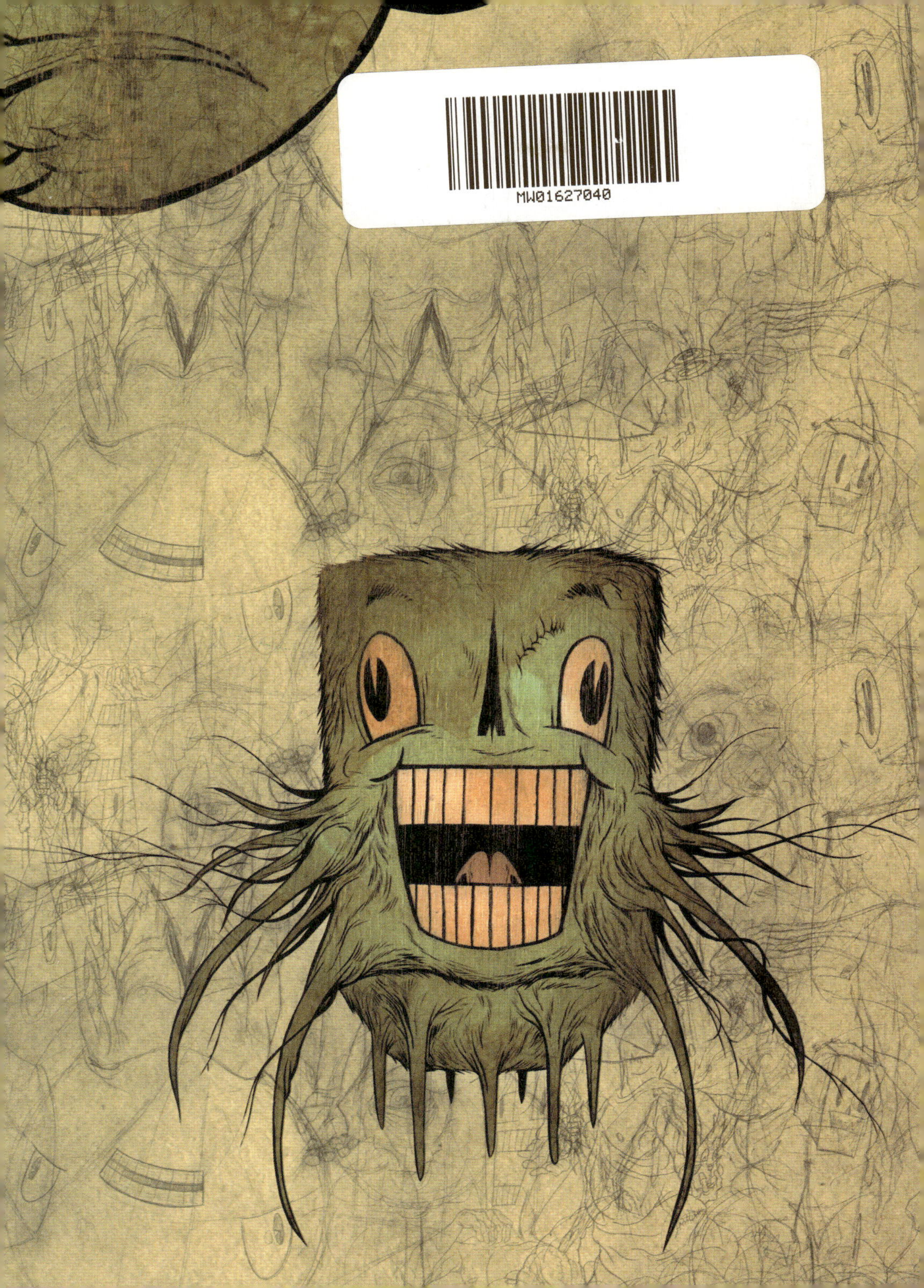

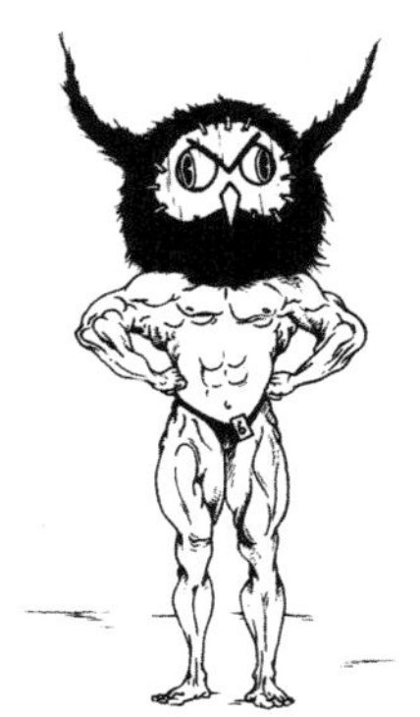

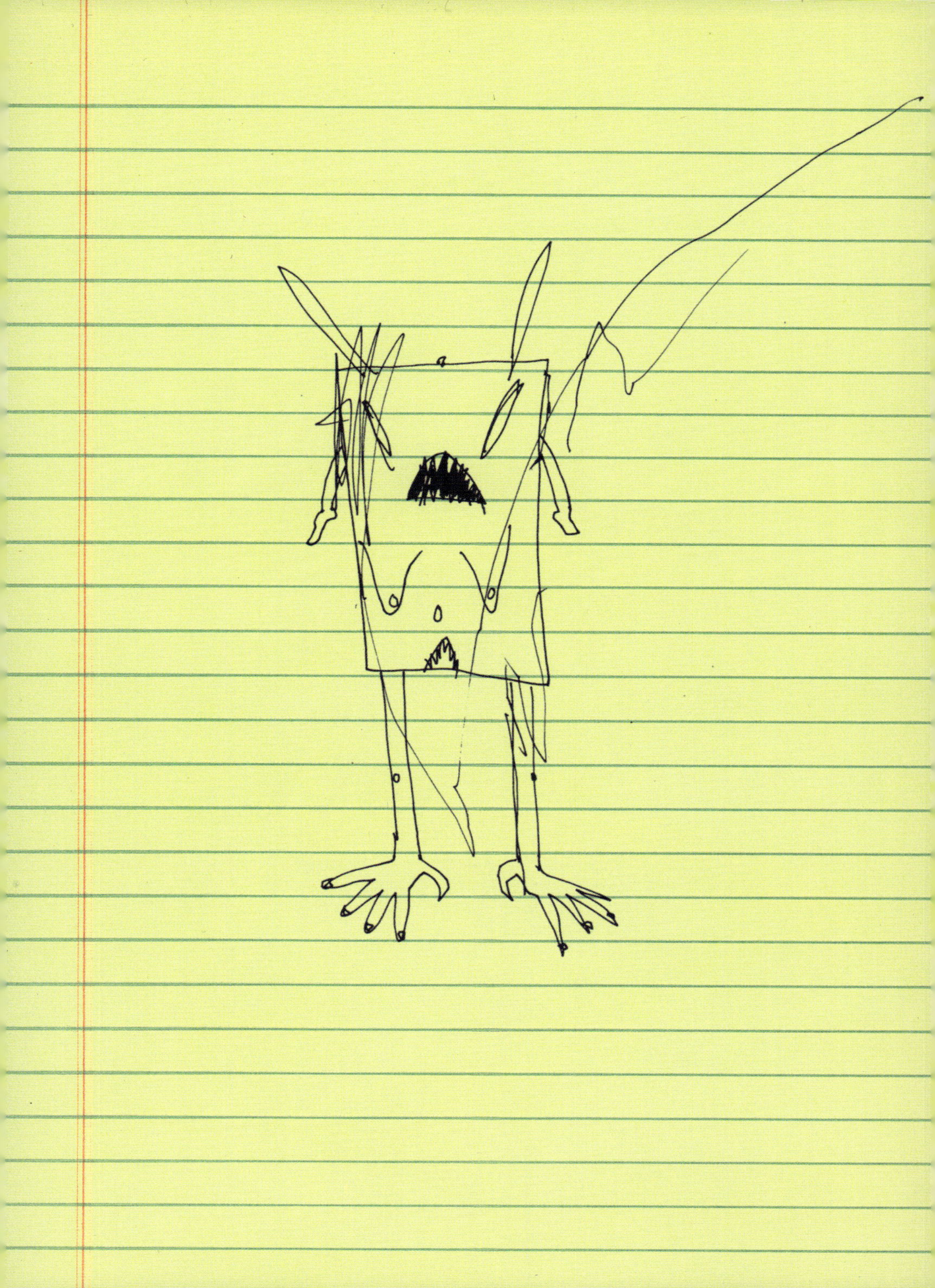

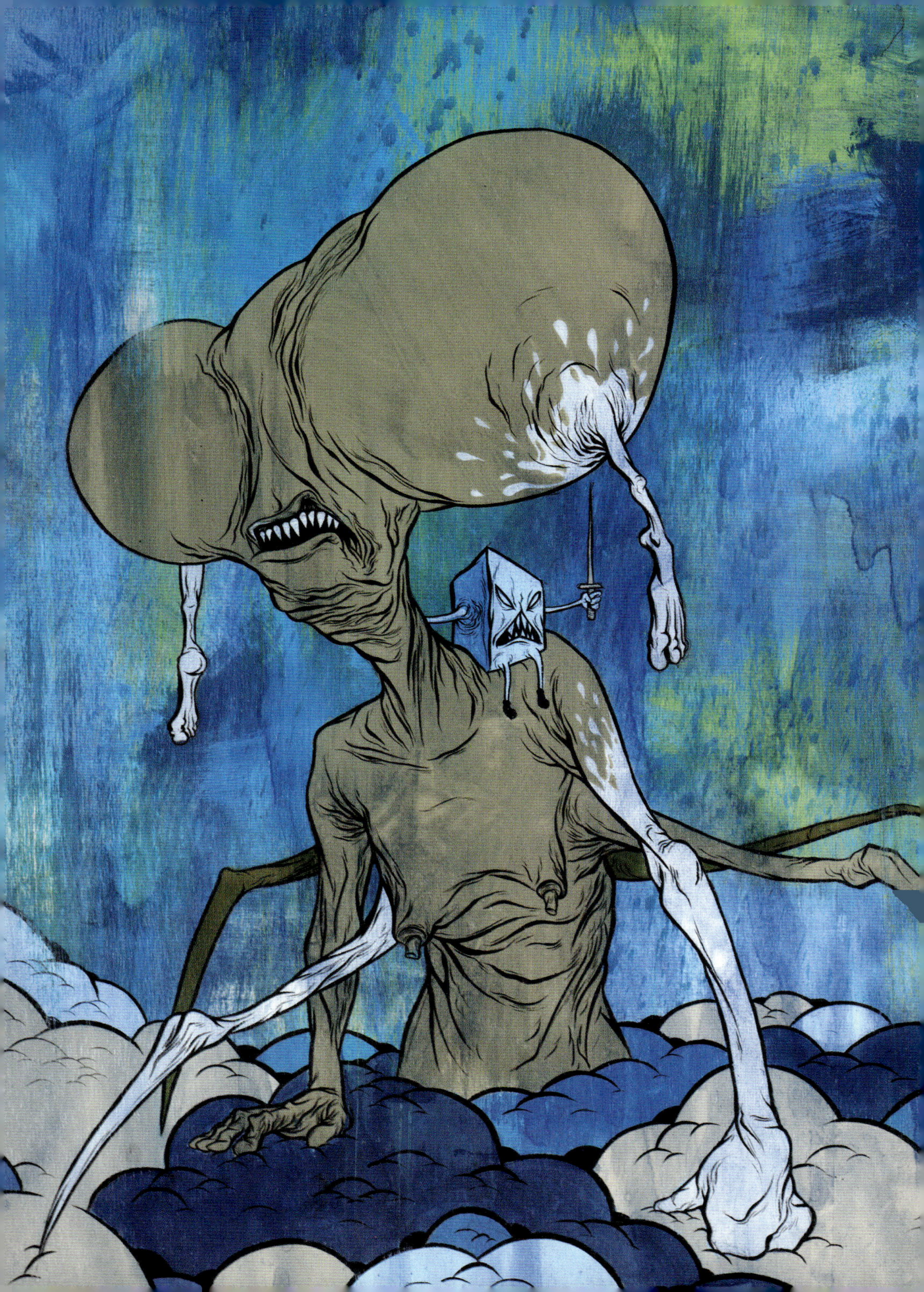

These pages will turn easy.

This is serious work. Crystal clear from the beginning is that this is one artist's distinct blazing path of dedication to the language of expression. The larger world of art and popular culture is in steady satellitic orbit outside this book; but this collection holds firm on it's own. For this is Earthbound and is heavy-metal and carries mass beyond the paper. This is the longitude and latitude of the path that has been forged by Alex Pardee's compass and coordinates alone. A bleeding edge visual exercise that passes above and below the folding nebulous corners of any school of art or ephemeral social movement. This is life as ink and medium. This is Alex Pardee.

These pages will make you grab someone close and pull him or her into your moment.

No part of this collection was born without a robotically precise hand and a focused wide open eye guiding it as images undulate and project from their visual plane. This here is all the missed calls of your life suddenly ringing you in one moment. This is smelling salts and cayenne; again, this is serious work. This is pots of gold and fables mixed with the syrup of television and the whispering allure of celebrity worship. This is bodies in awkward personal moments, this is grins and cringes, this is binges and self-imposed exiles. This is Alex Pardee.

You want to see what is perched ahead, what lies within and what is waiting to be articulated in flickers of visual metaphor and sentiment on the next page. This is a peering lens into that strange space one finds as they emerge from sleep but still loosely hold the tendrils of dreams. The shape shifting and faces, the colors retreating into texture, motions halted, metamorphosis forward and backward, disguised agendas, anxious grief and exaltation. This is happy faced life in states of fission and fusion, cuisine and nausea, noses and teeth, business and pleasure.

In these pages is the sense of arrival and as you turn you will find yourself trying to remember the details, maybe re-tracing the projecting figures' silhouettes in your palms, or trying to see the inspiration behind the spectacle, or simply trying to know what tools were employed in its crafting. The stitches and shading, the wrinkles and canyons of folding skin; all serving as a gift-wrap to something that shakes and shudders as if seeing light for the first time. You may hear the pen bleeding itself onto surfaces and the not so distant pendulum behind ticking and tocking and telling this artist to finish just one more piece. Alex both hears and heeds the ticking, and that means that soon you will have the chance to see it.

For right now, turn these pages, for these will be the first turns in a long and omni-directional spiraling course that if you let it will take you places oddly familiar but described in a language as strikingly new as it is satisfying to absorb.

Written by Alex's friend Jeben Berg - January 2008

"At night I can't sleep,
I toss and turn,
Candlesticks in the dark,
Visions of bodies being burned."
– Scarface of the
Geto Boys
"My Mind's Playin
Tricks on Me"
1991

220 Fillmore Street, San Francisco, CA 94117
phone 415.252.0144 fax 415.252.1482
www.upperplayground.com
www.fifty24sf.com

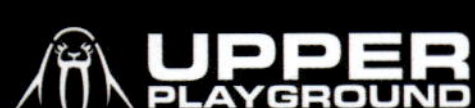

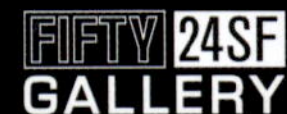

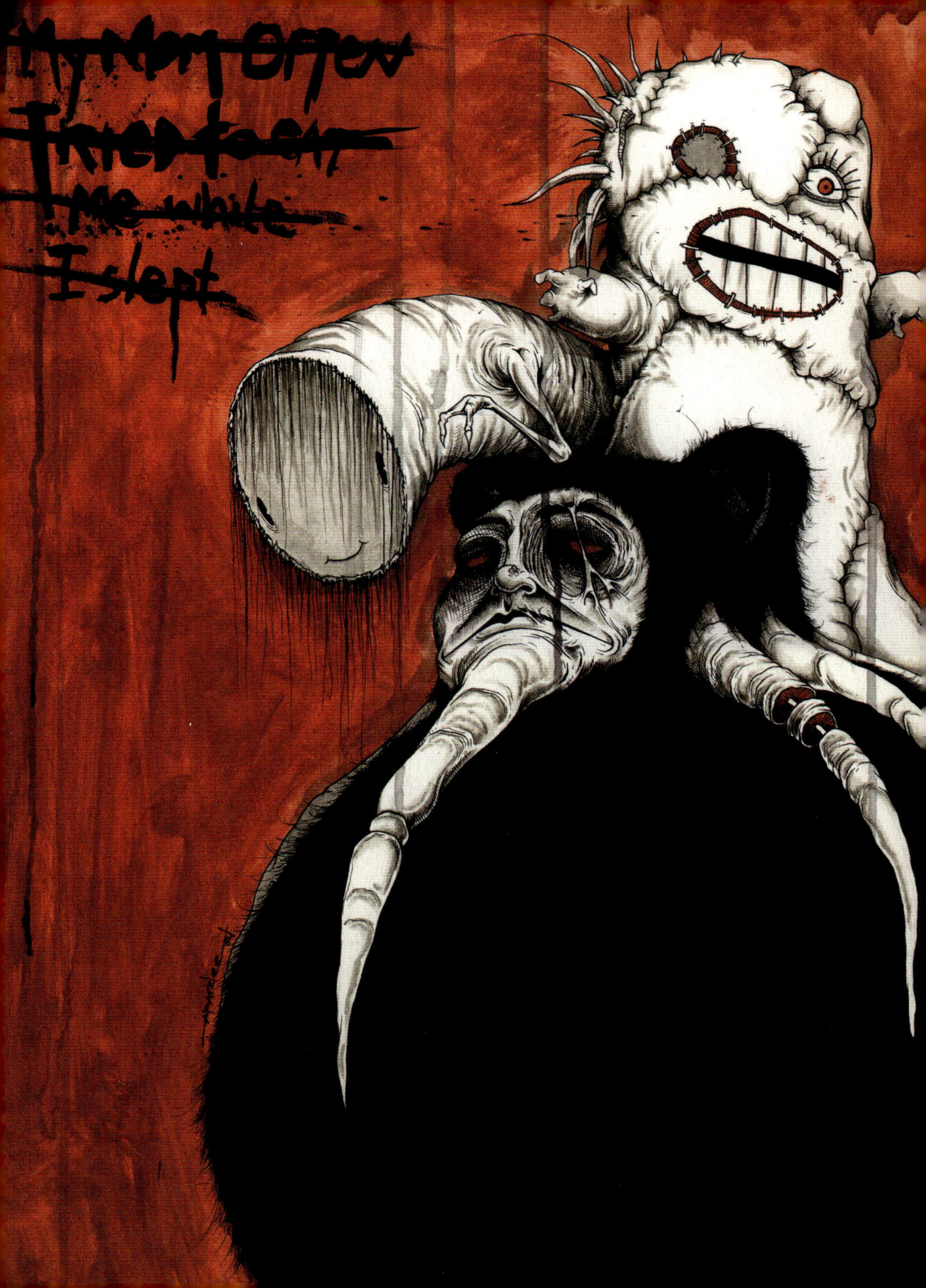
My Mom Often
Tried to eat
me while
I slept

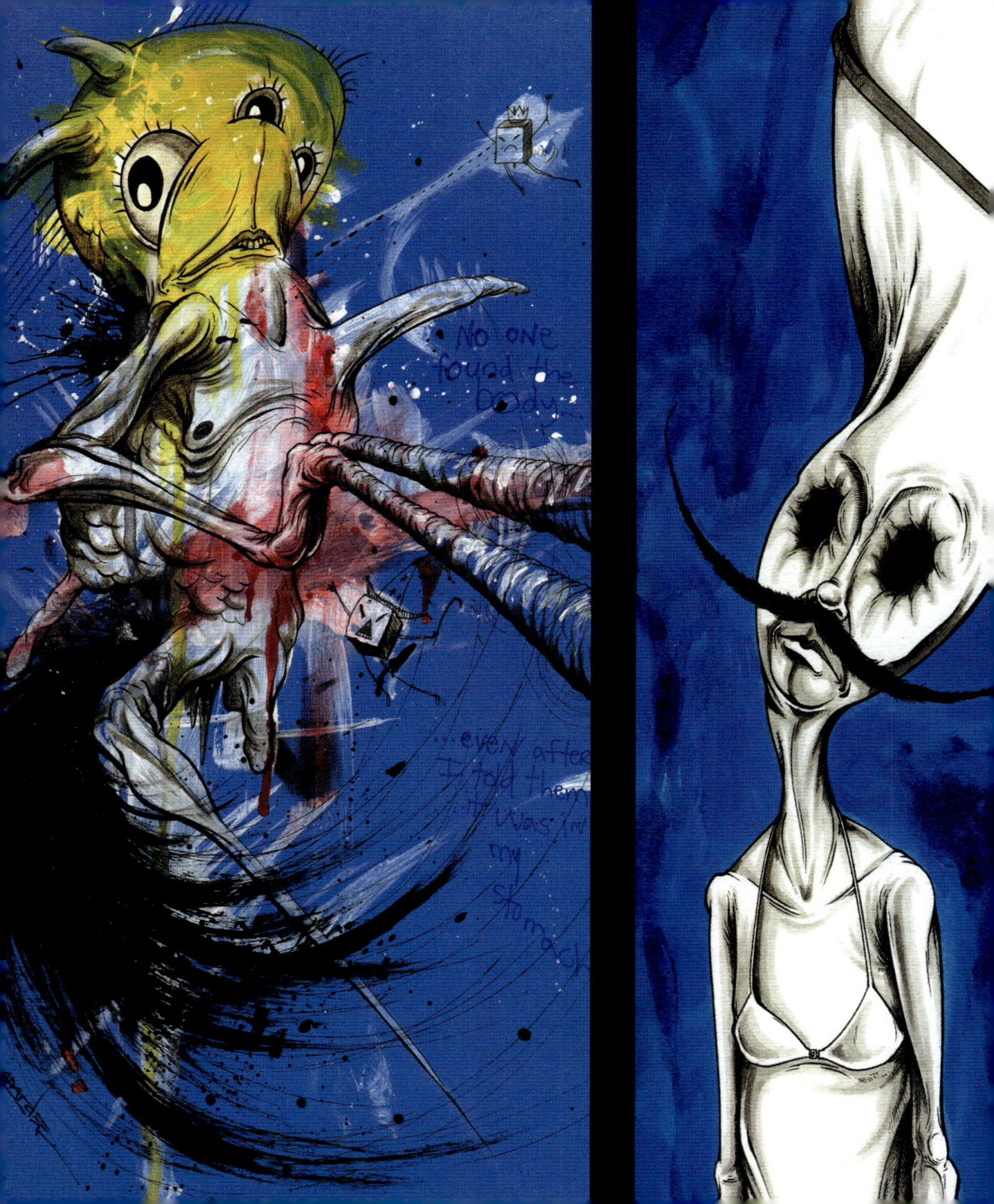
No one found the body...
...even after I told them it was in my stomach

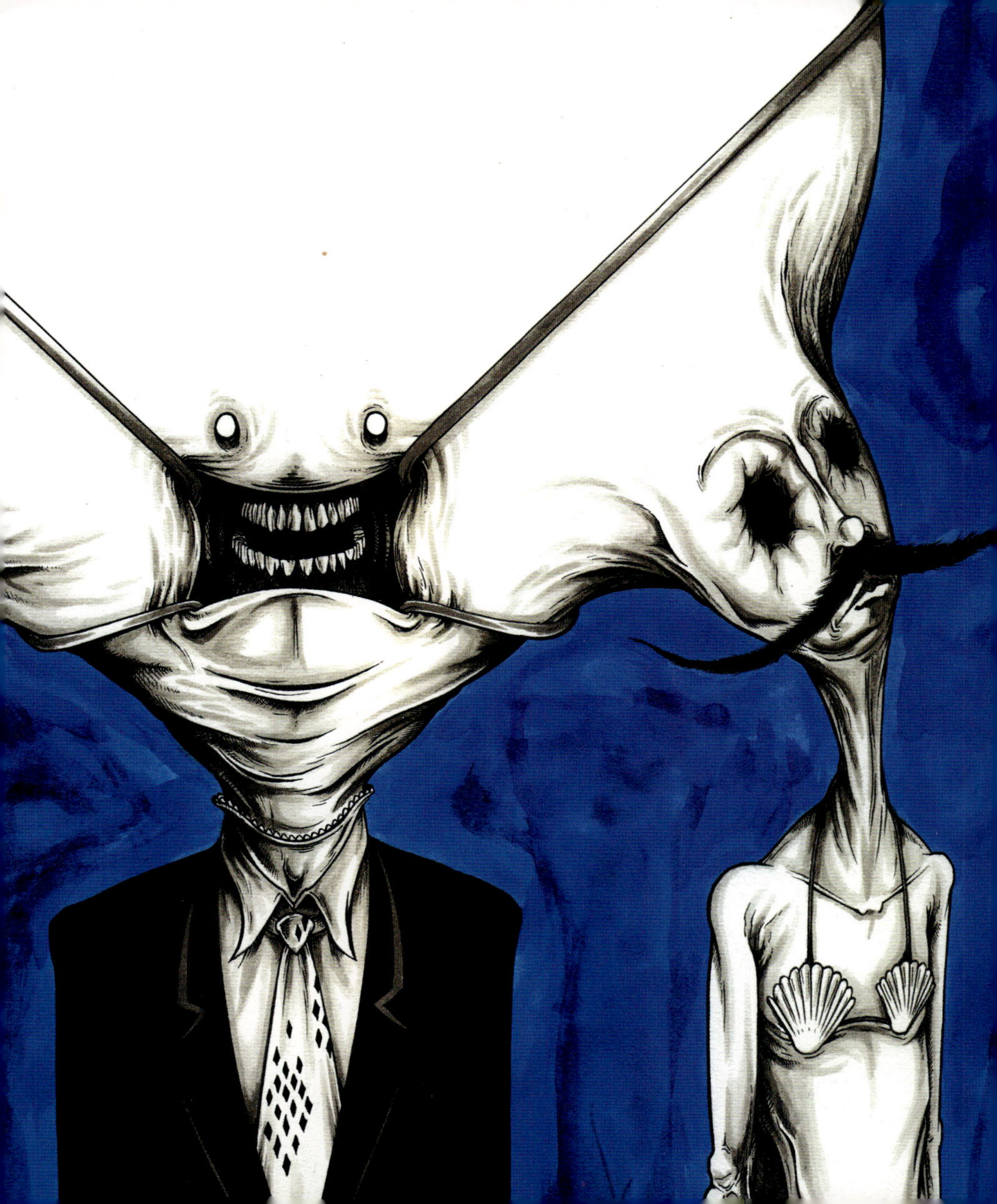

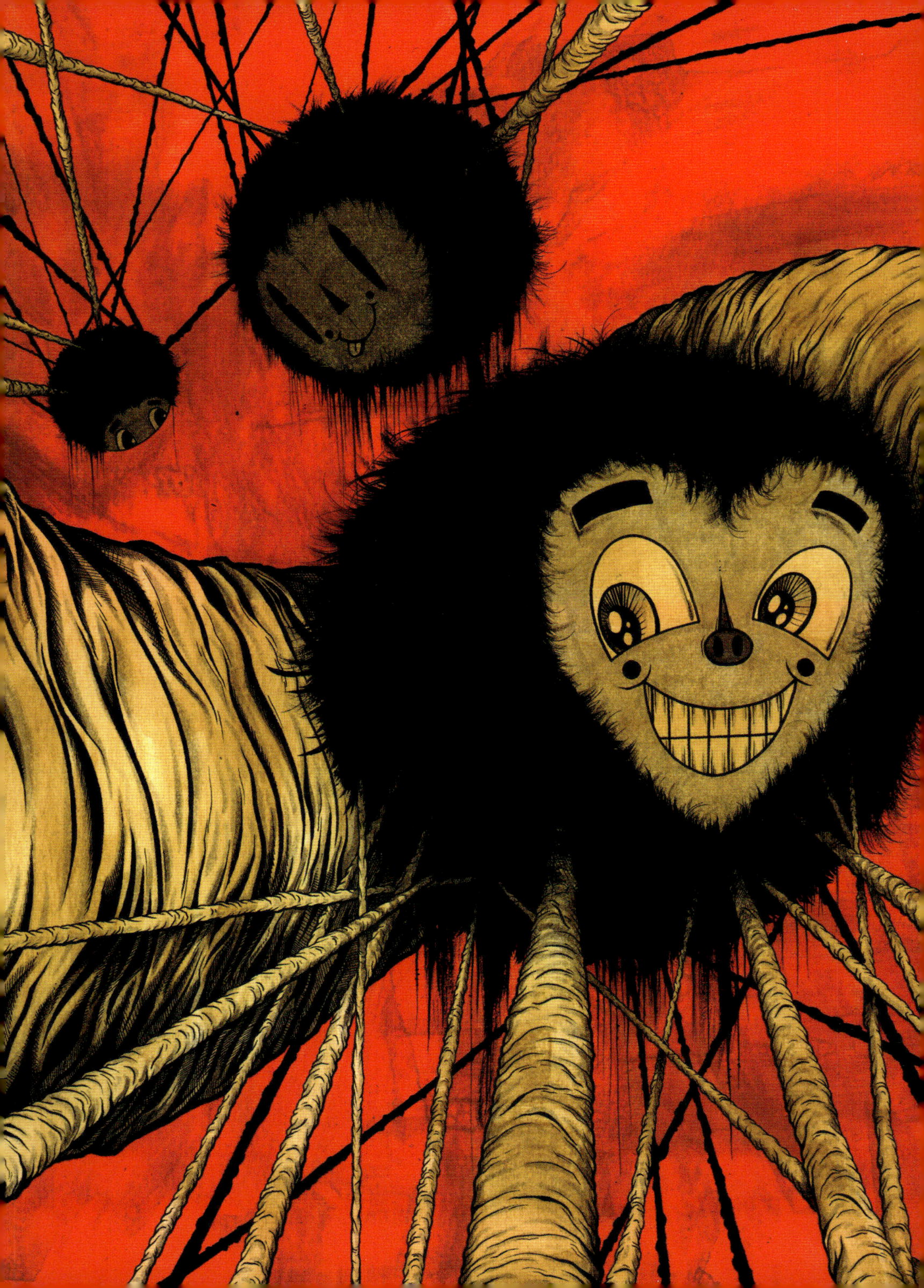

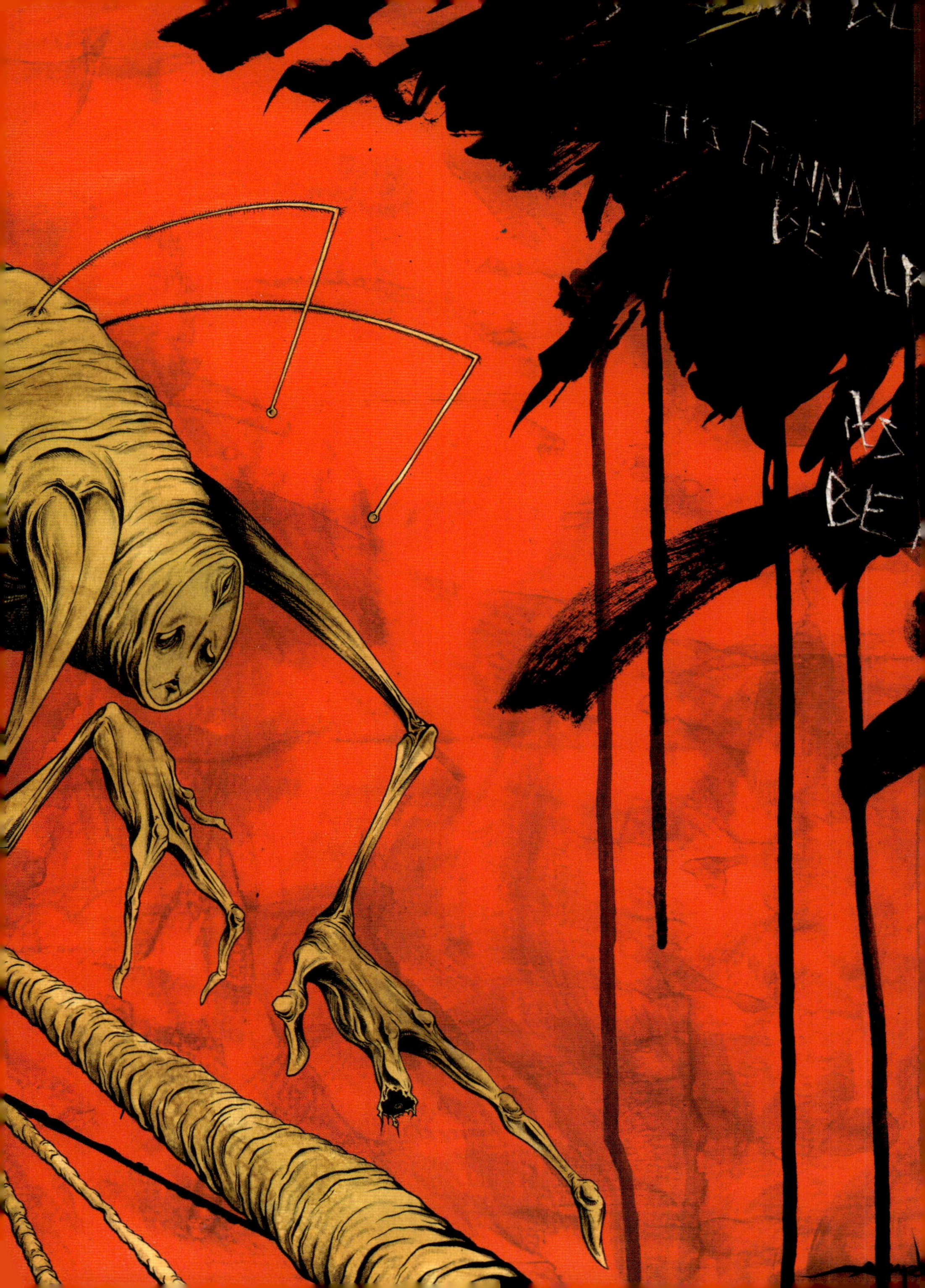

ITS GONNA
BE
ITS
BE

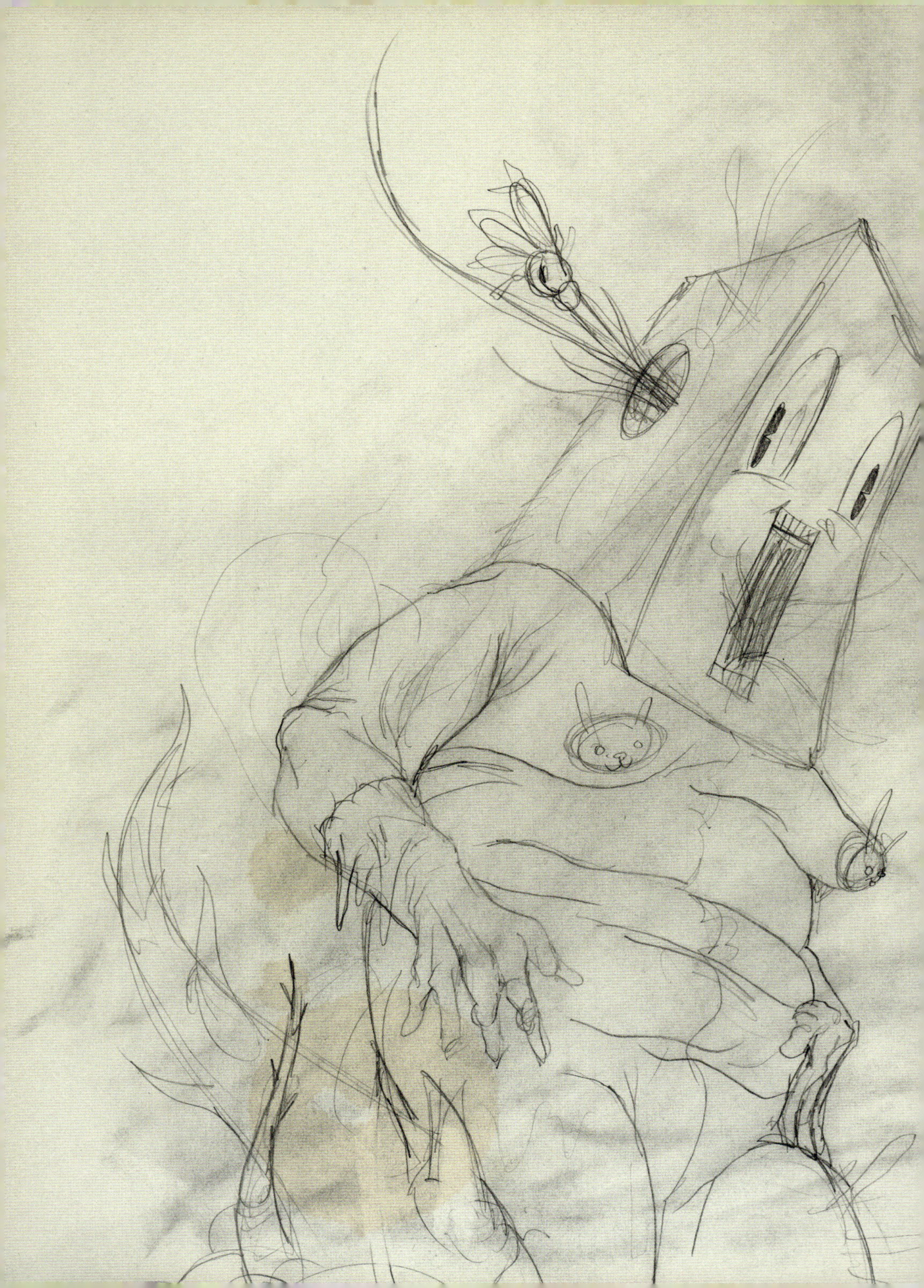

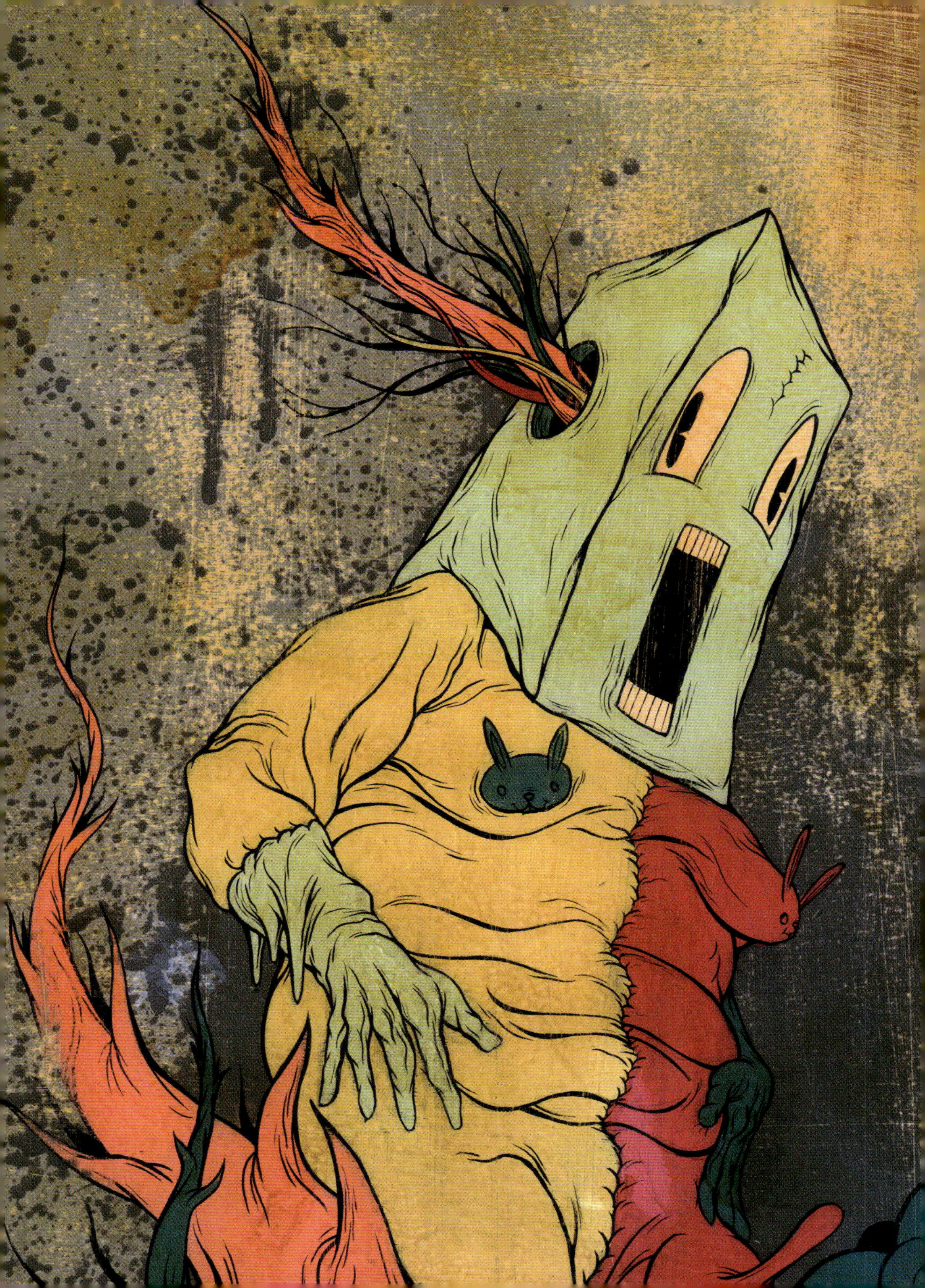

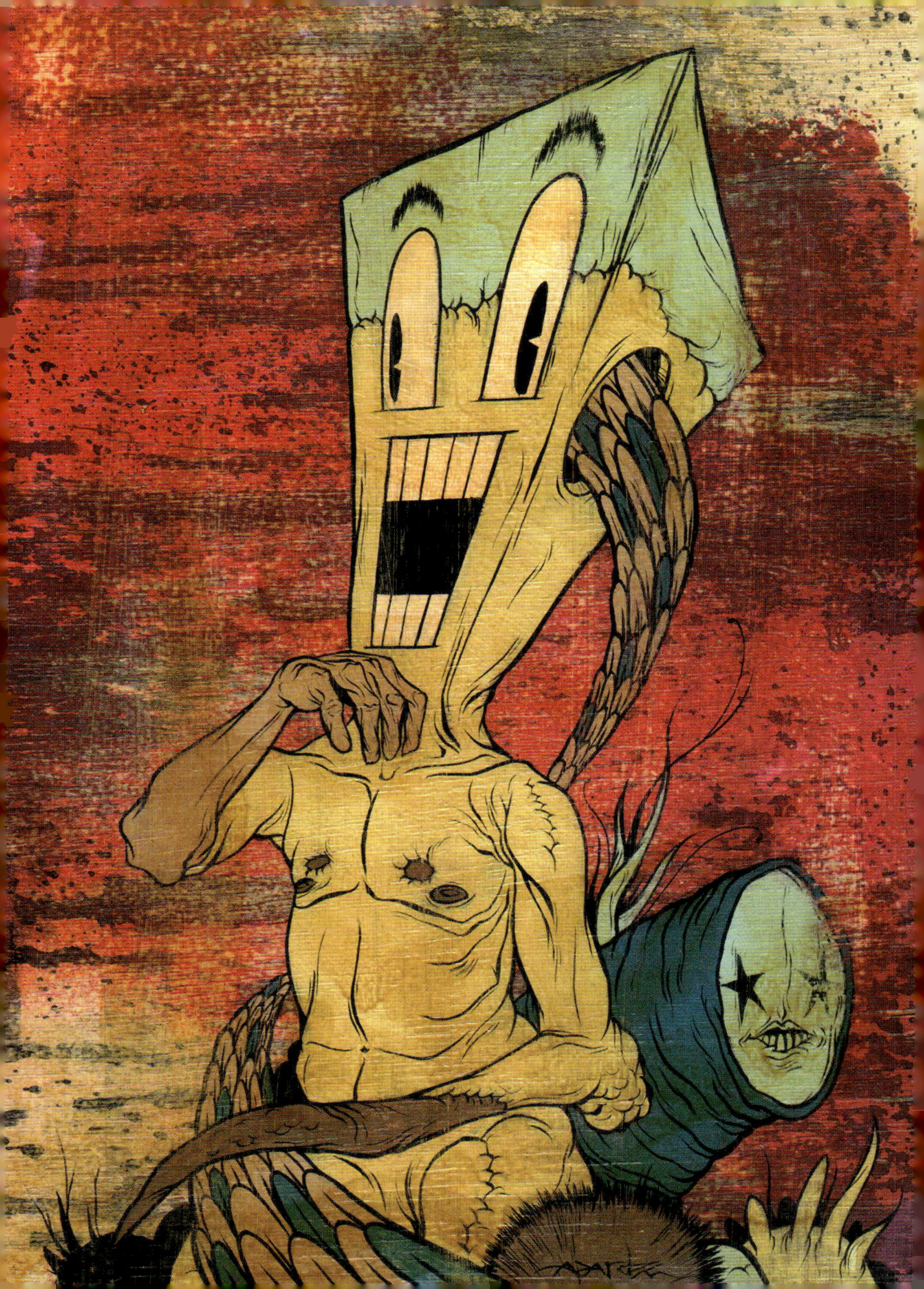

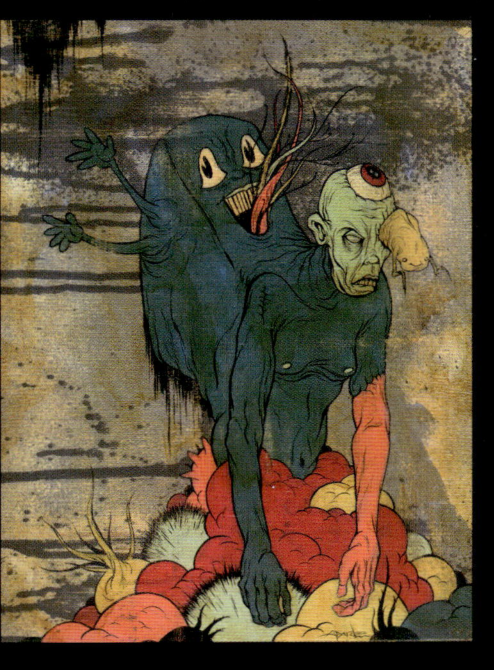

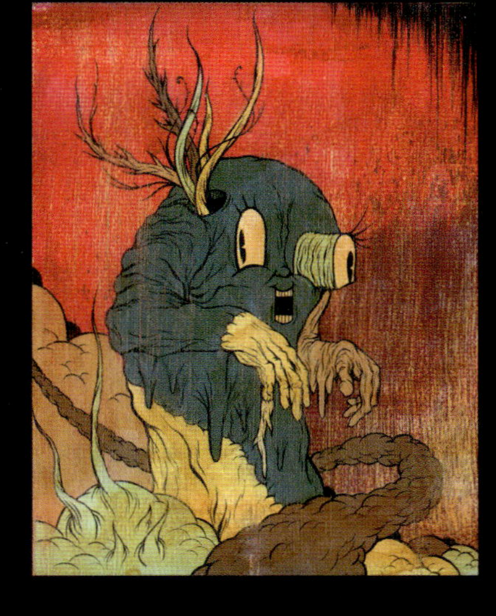

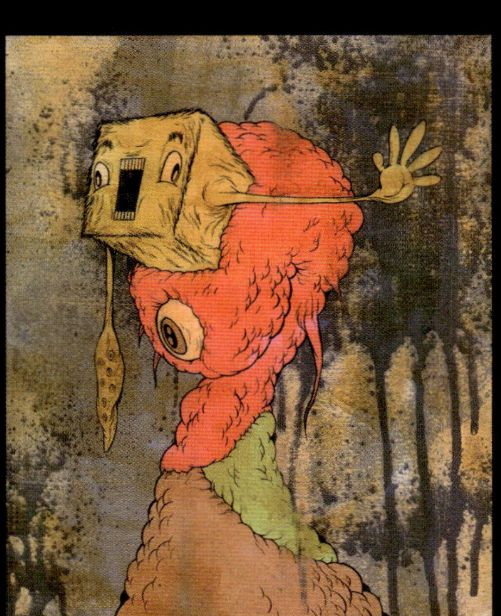

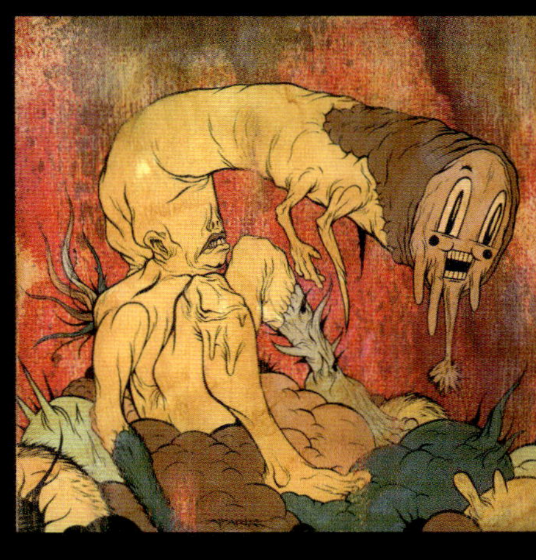

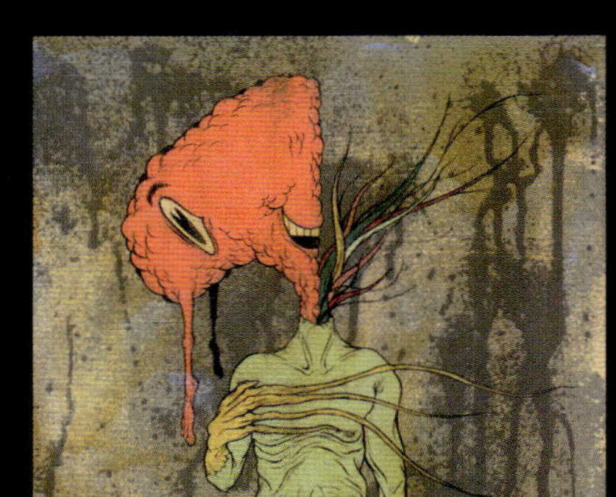

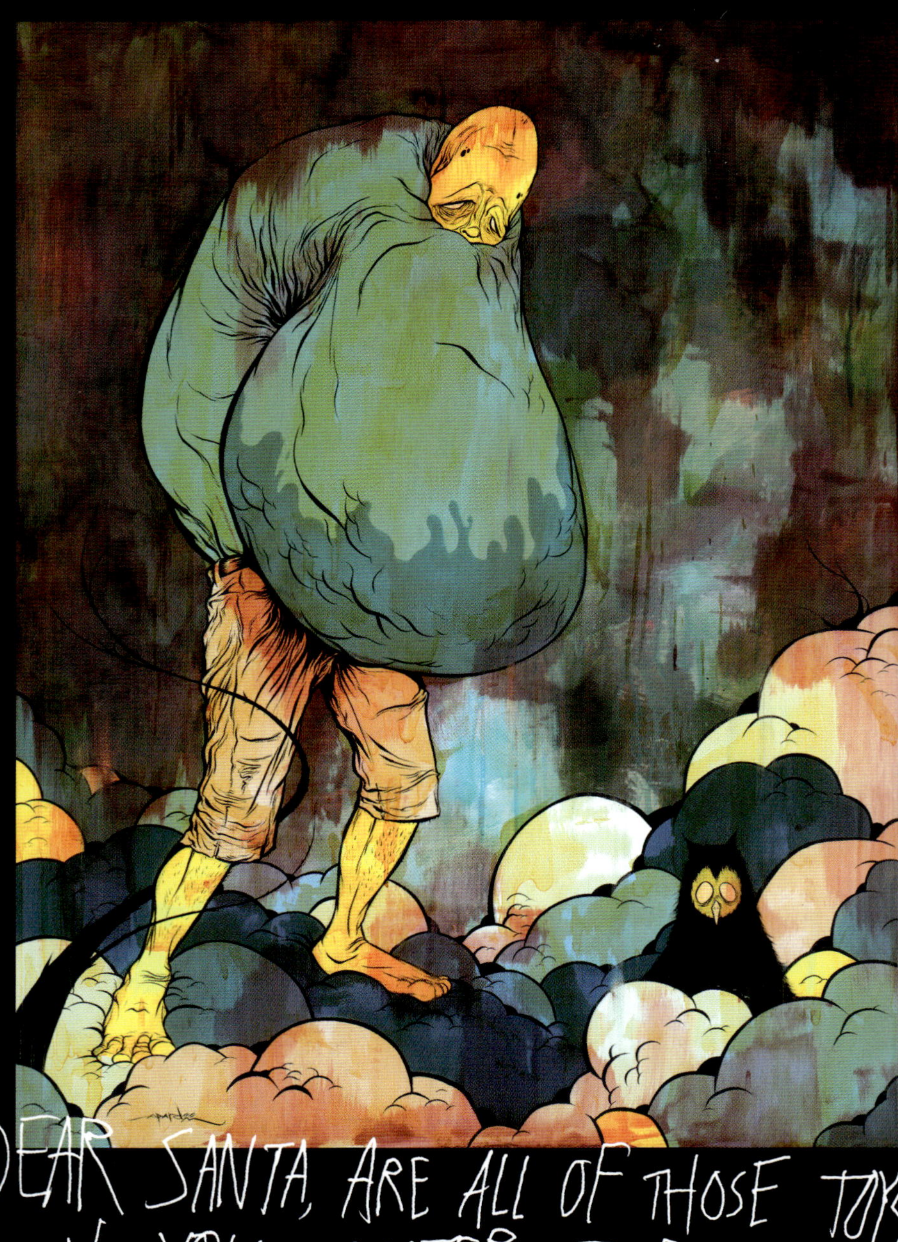

DEAR SANTA, ARE ALL OF THOSE TOYS
IN YOUR GOITER FOR ME?

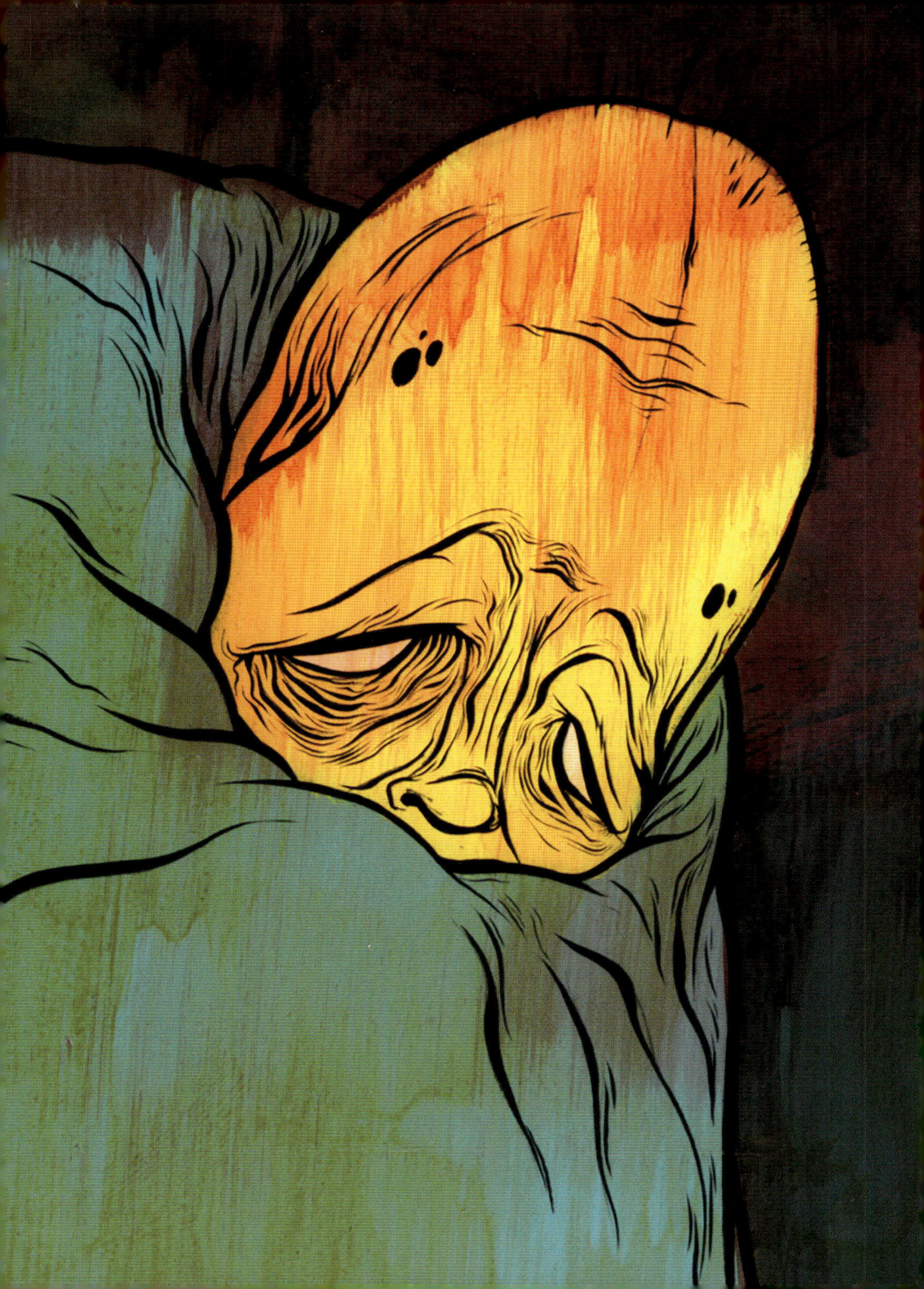

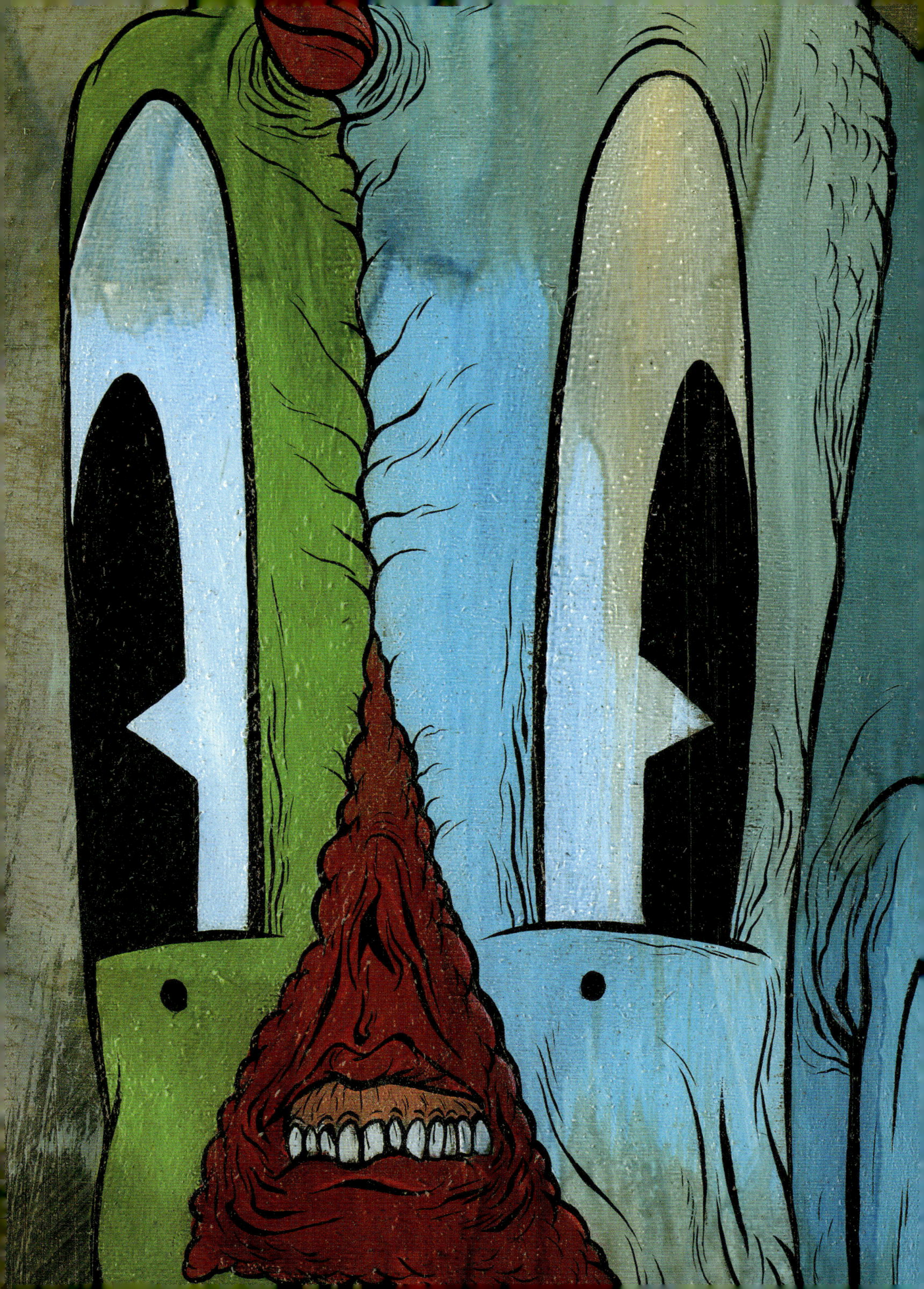

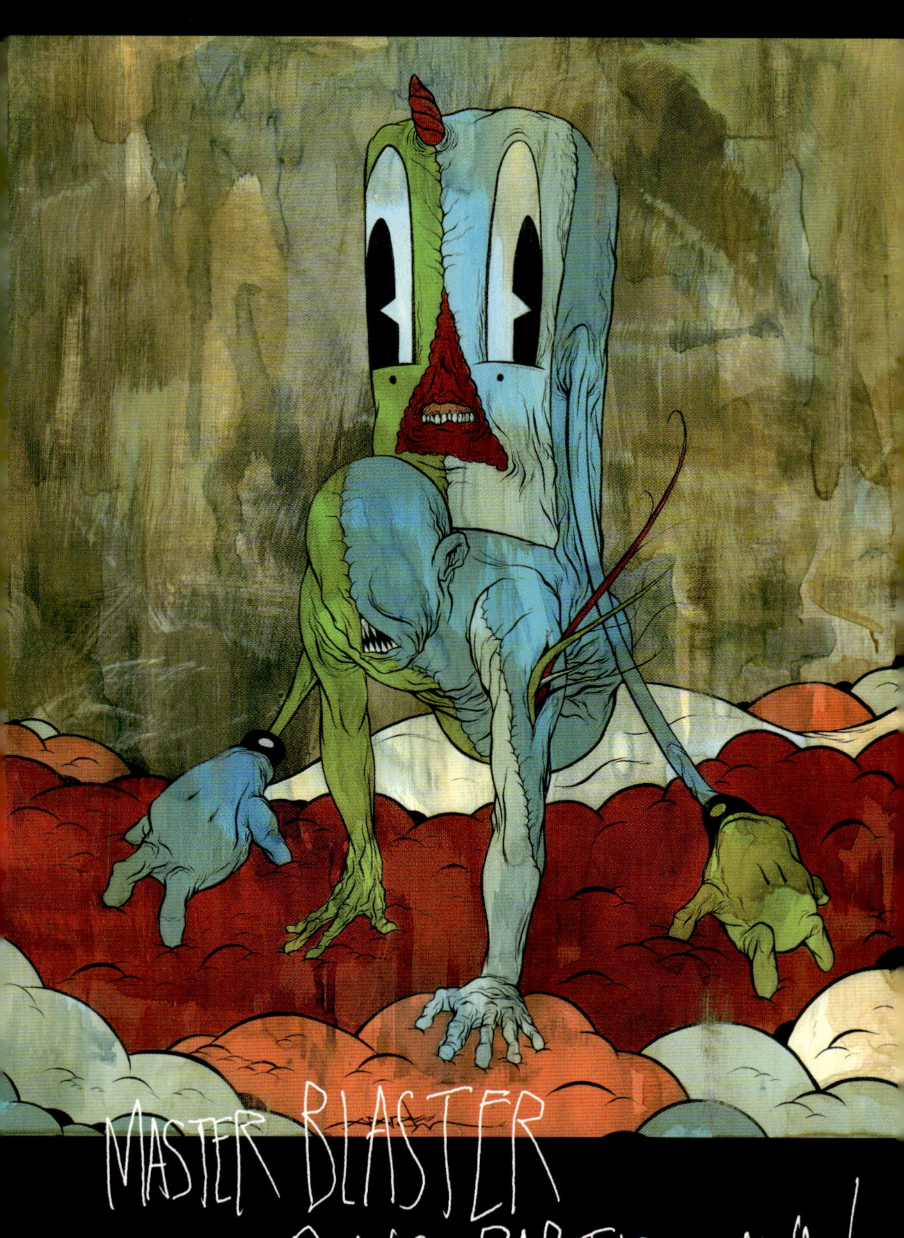

MASTER BLASTER
RUNS BARTERTOWN

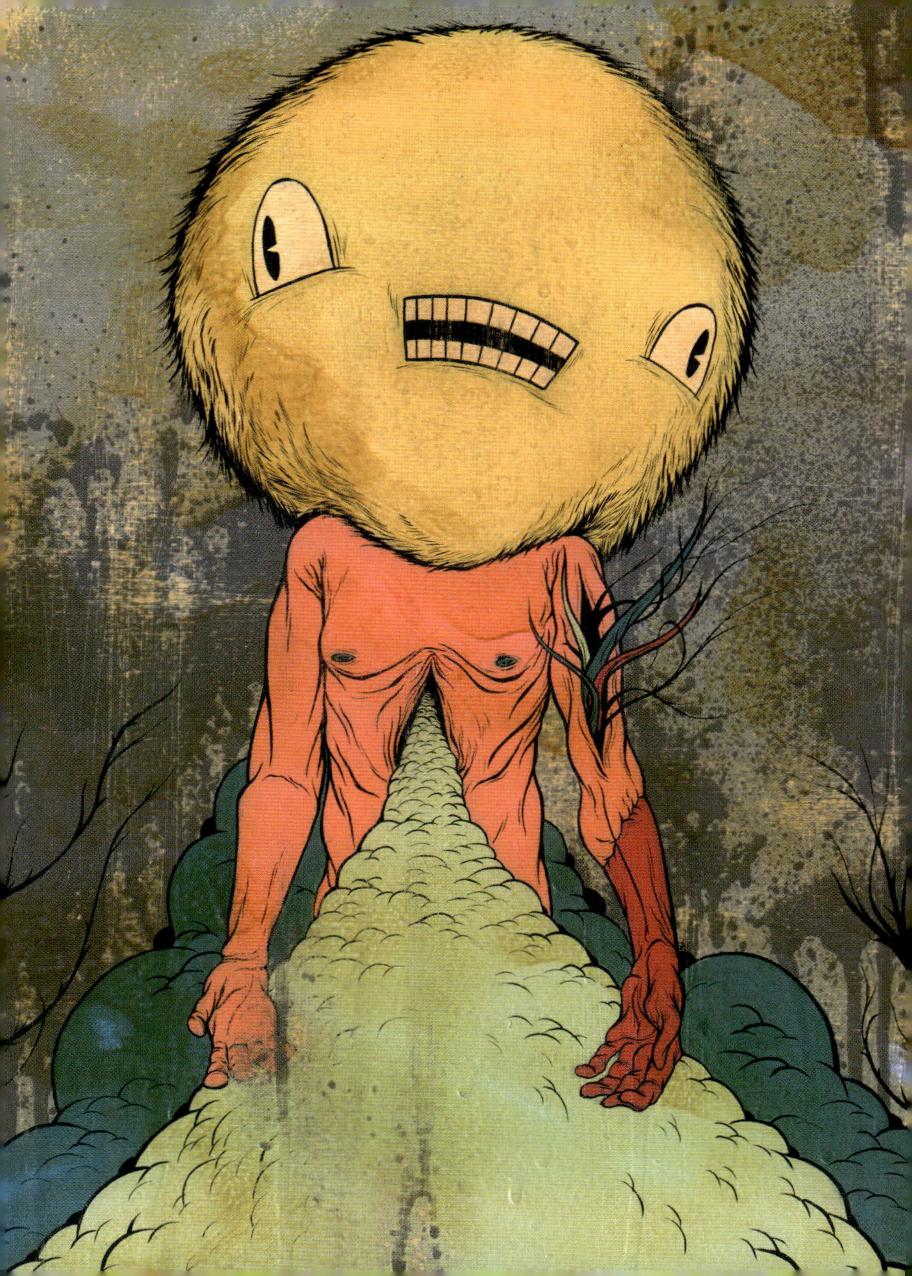

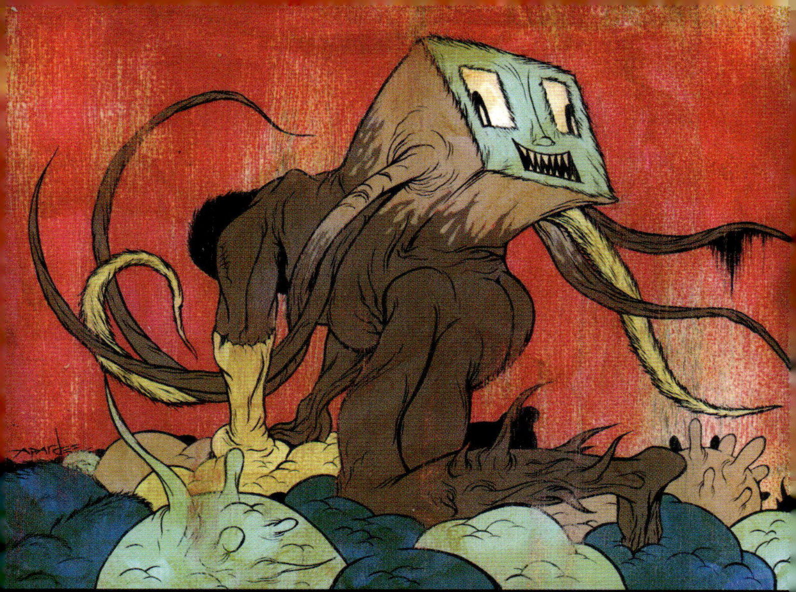

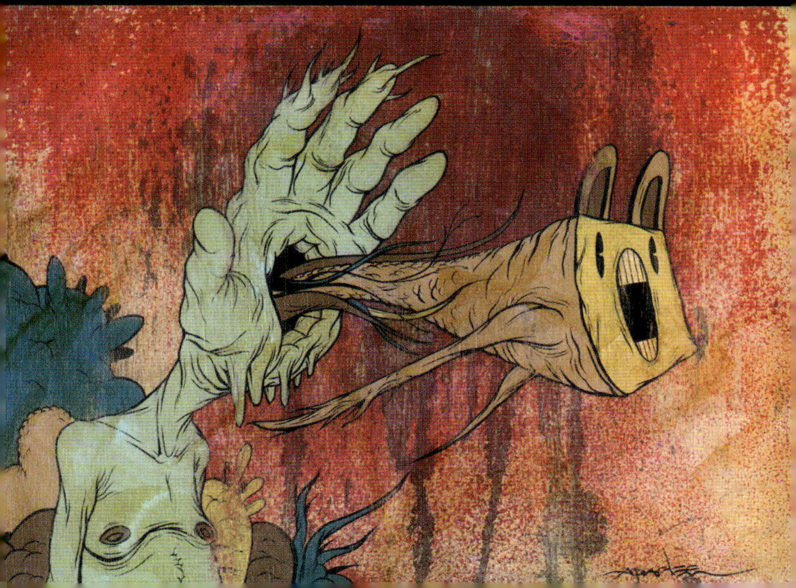

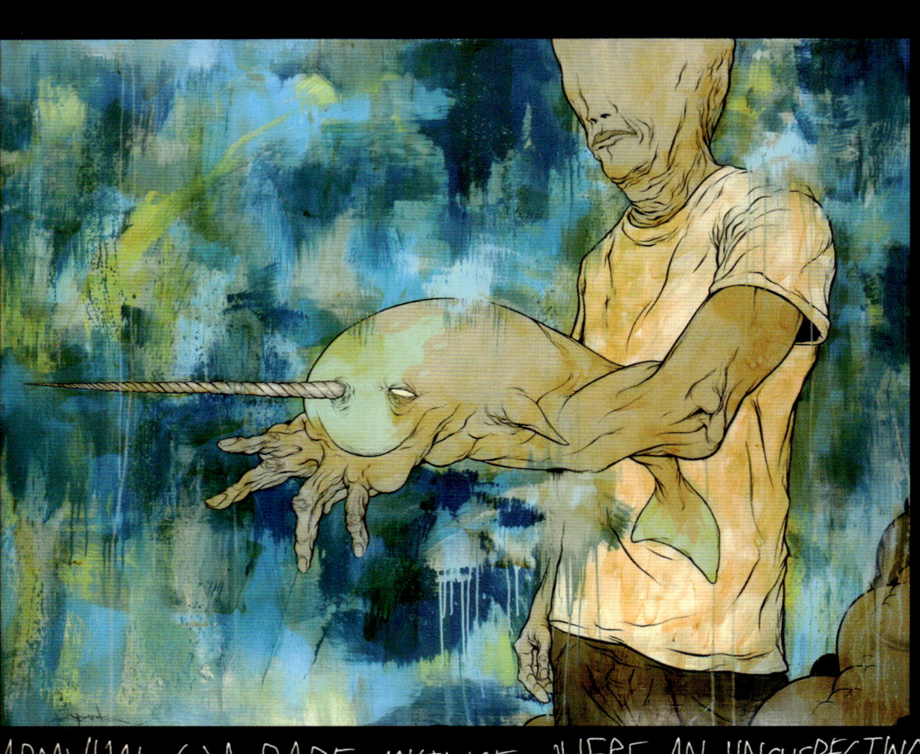

ARMWHAL: (1) A RARE INSTANCE WHERE AN UNSUSPECTING PERSON'S ARM BEGINS MORPHING INTO A NARWHAL, ONE OF THE MOST FASCINATING OF ALL THE ARCTIC WHALES.

ARMWHAL: (2) THE GREATEST WEAPON EVER.*

*EVEN BETTER THAN WOLVERINE

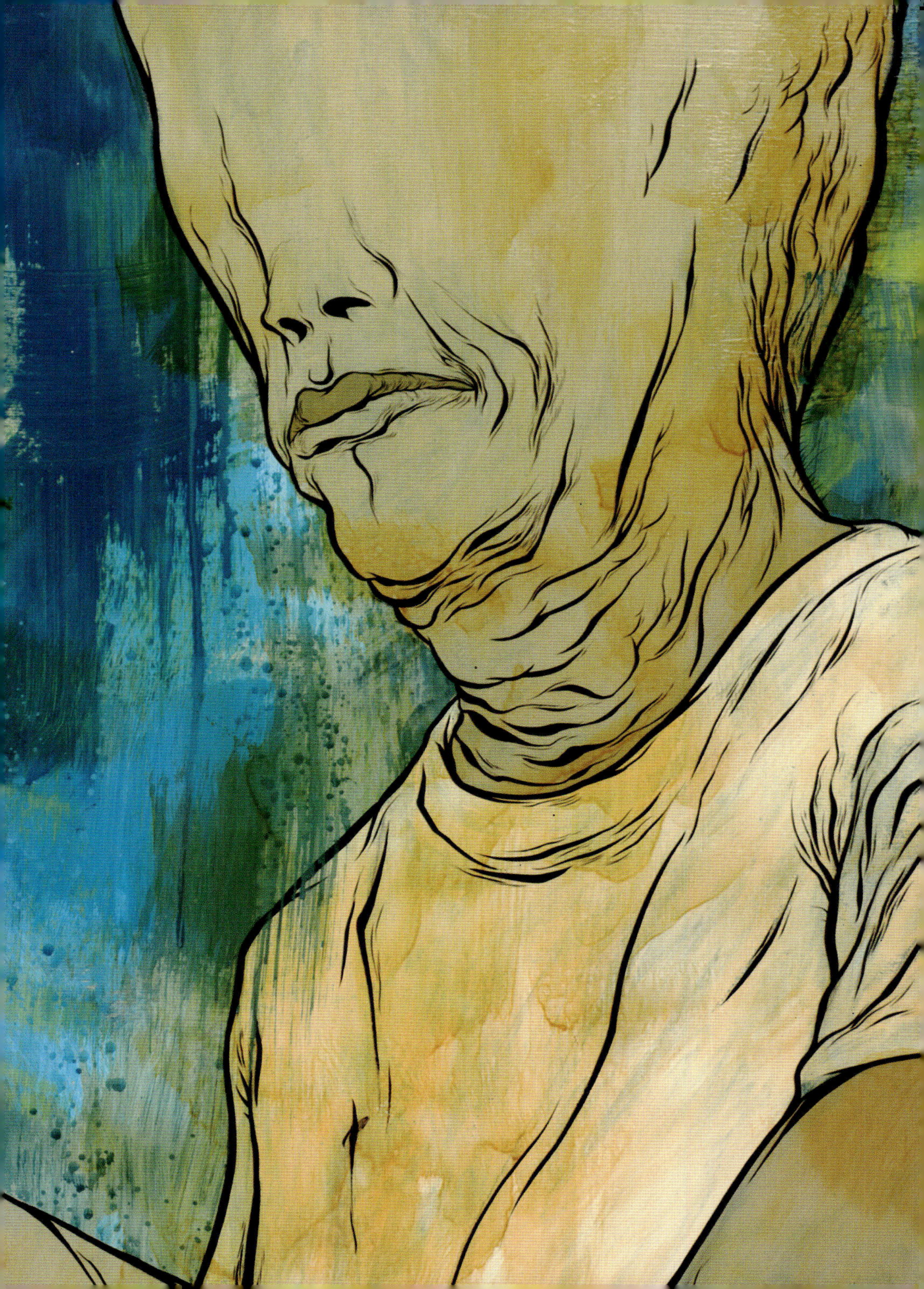

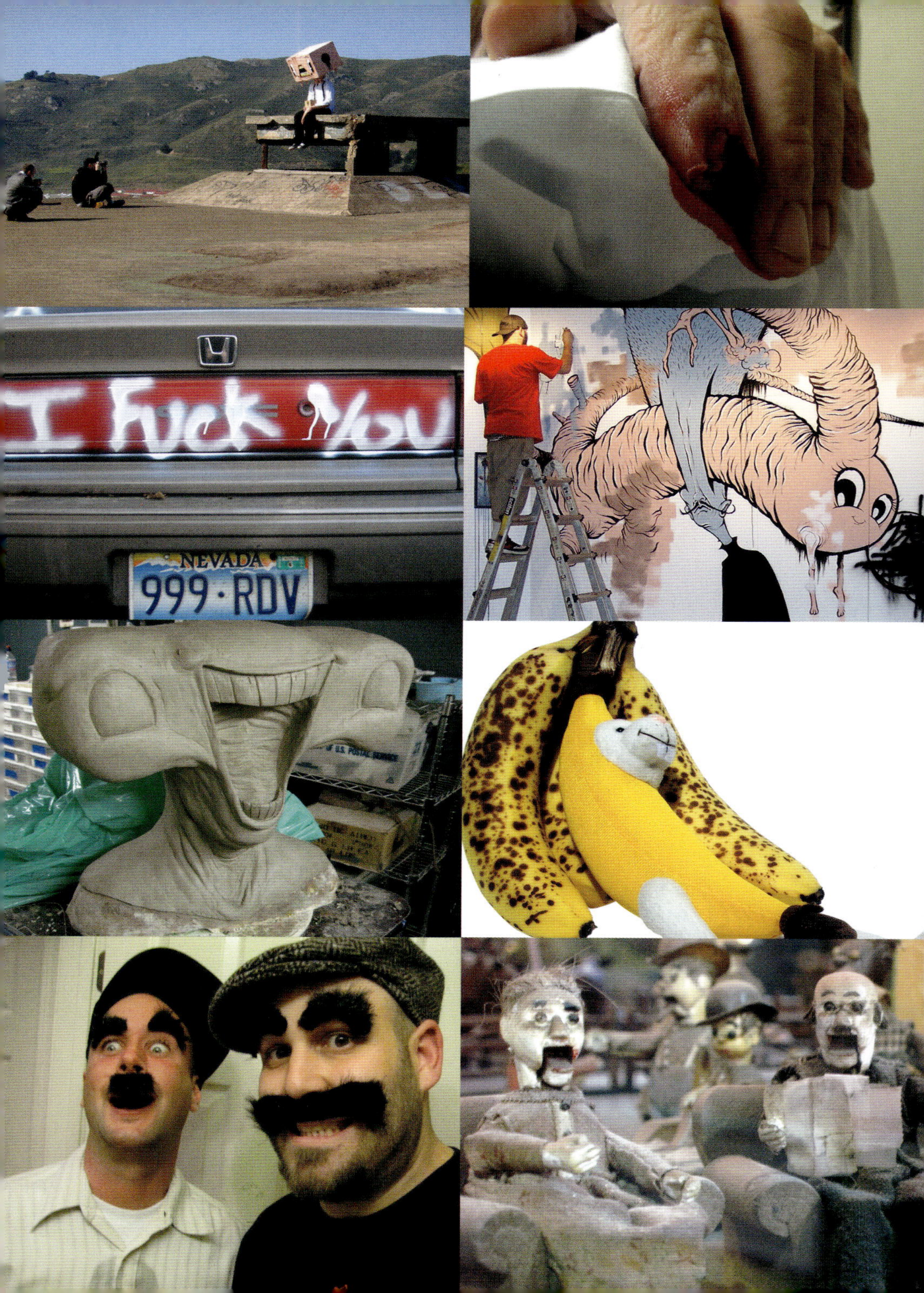
I Fuck You
NEVADA
999·RDV

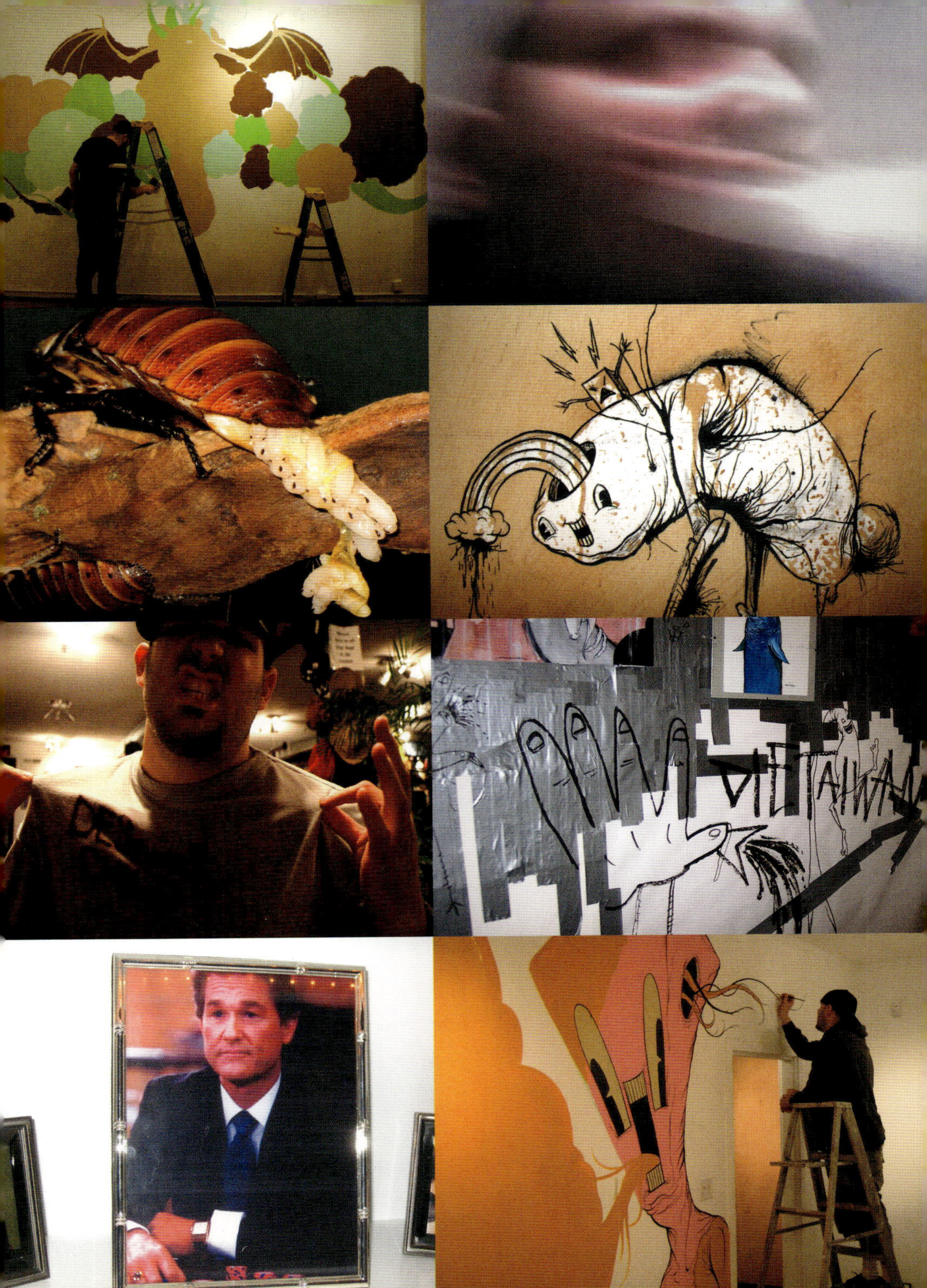

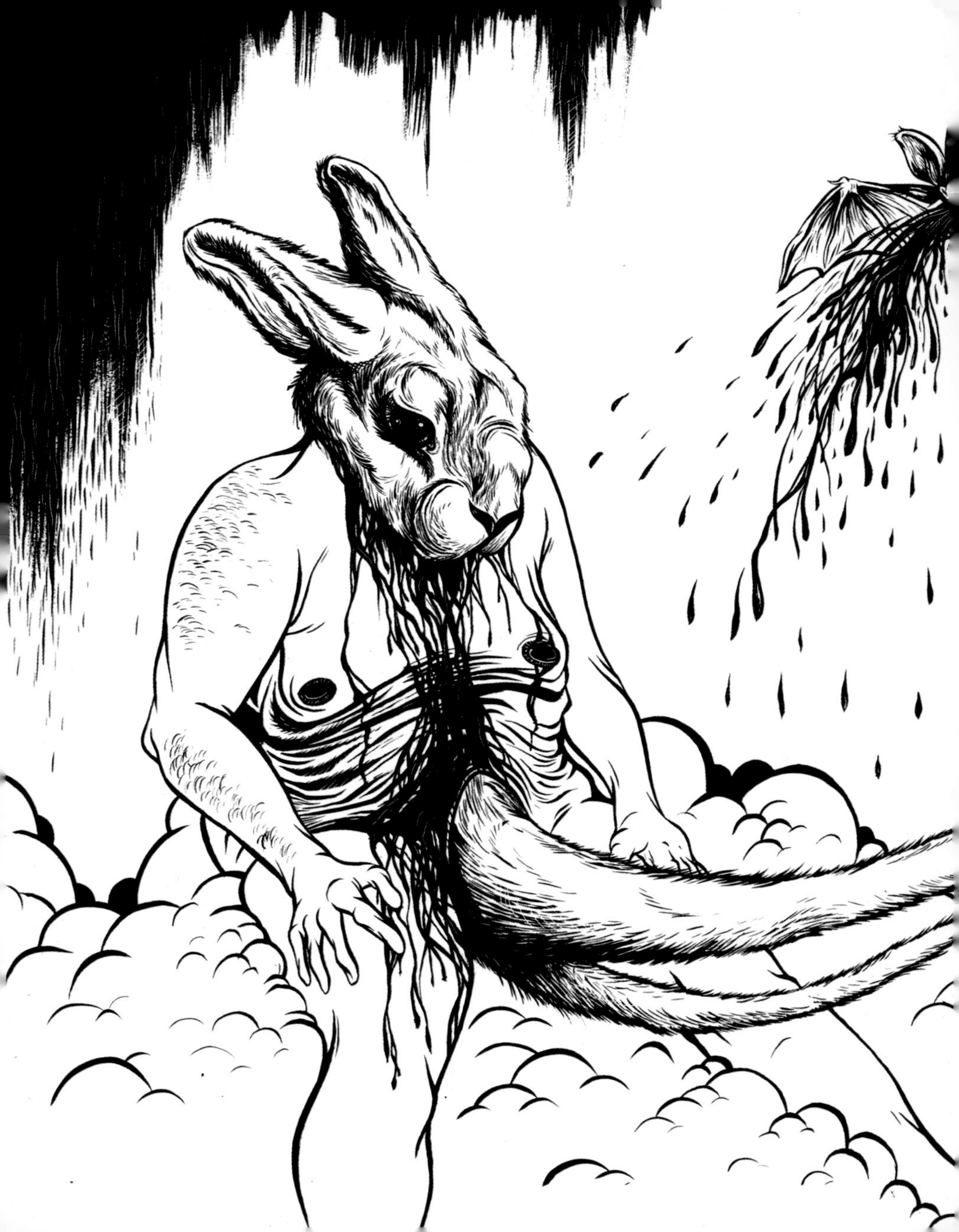

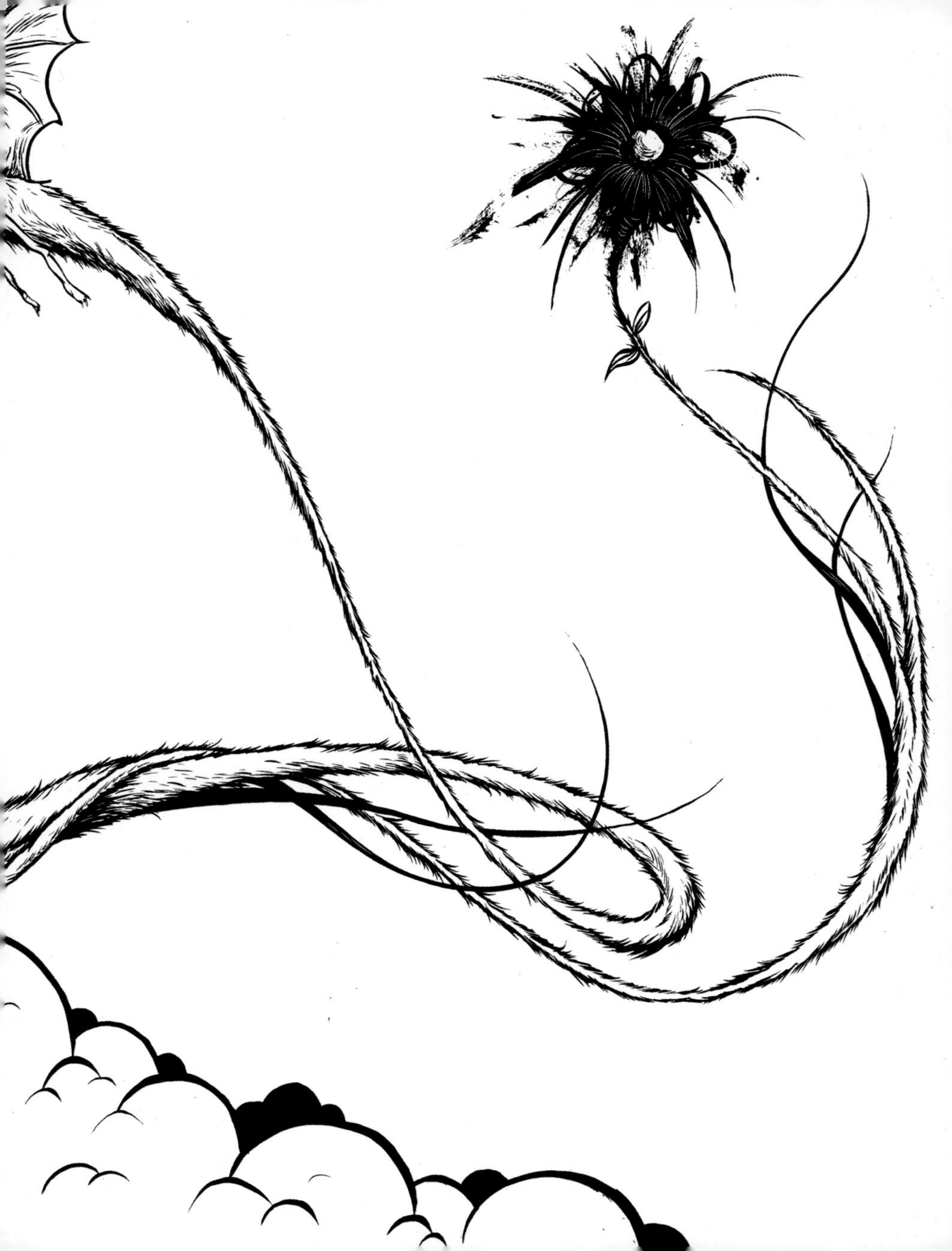

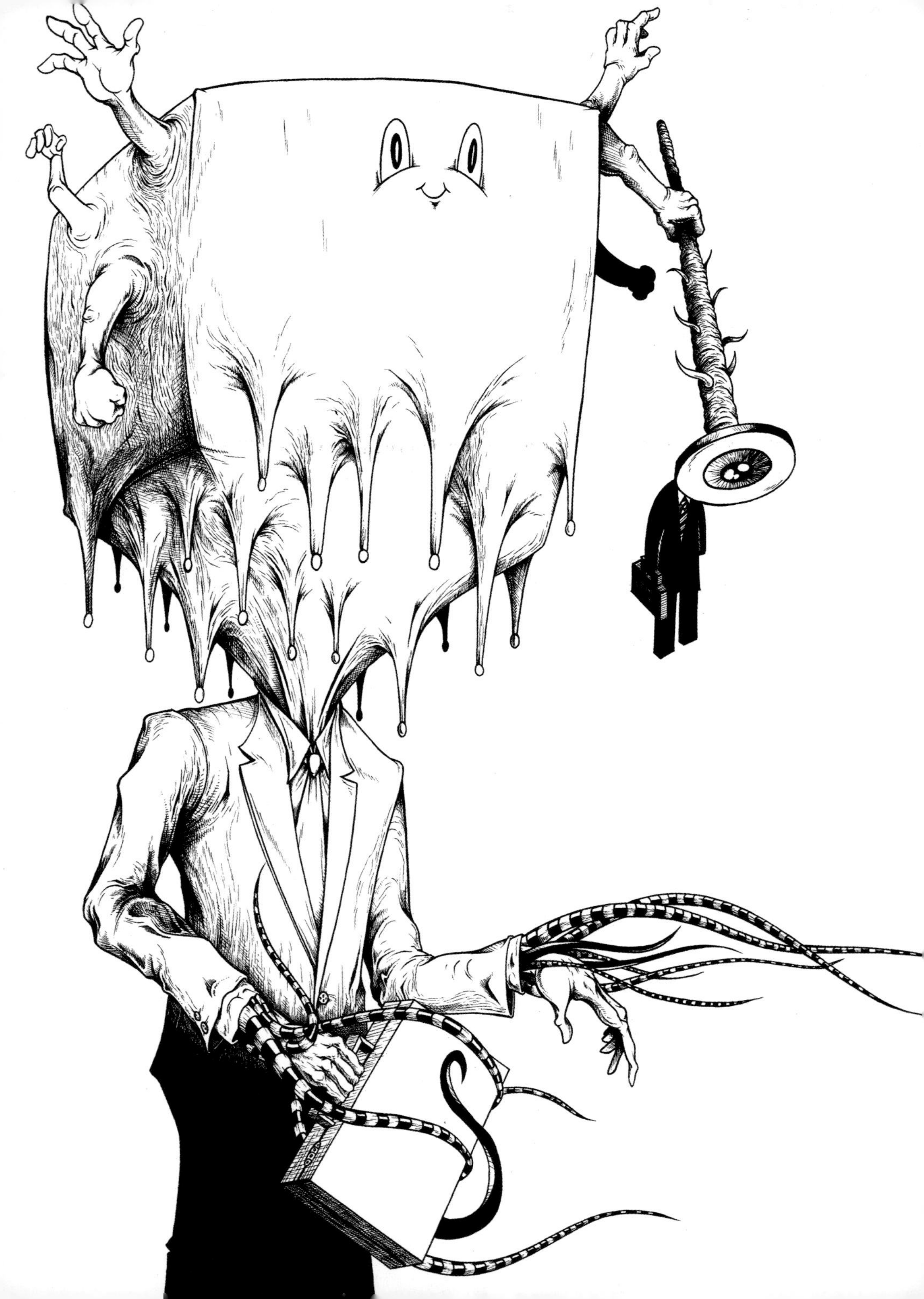

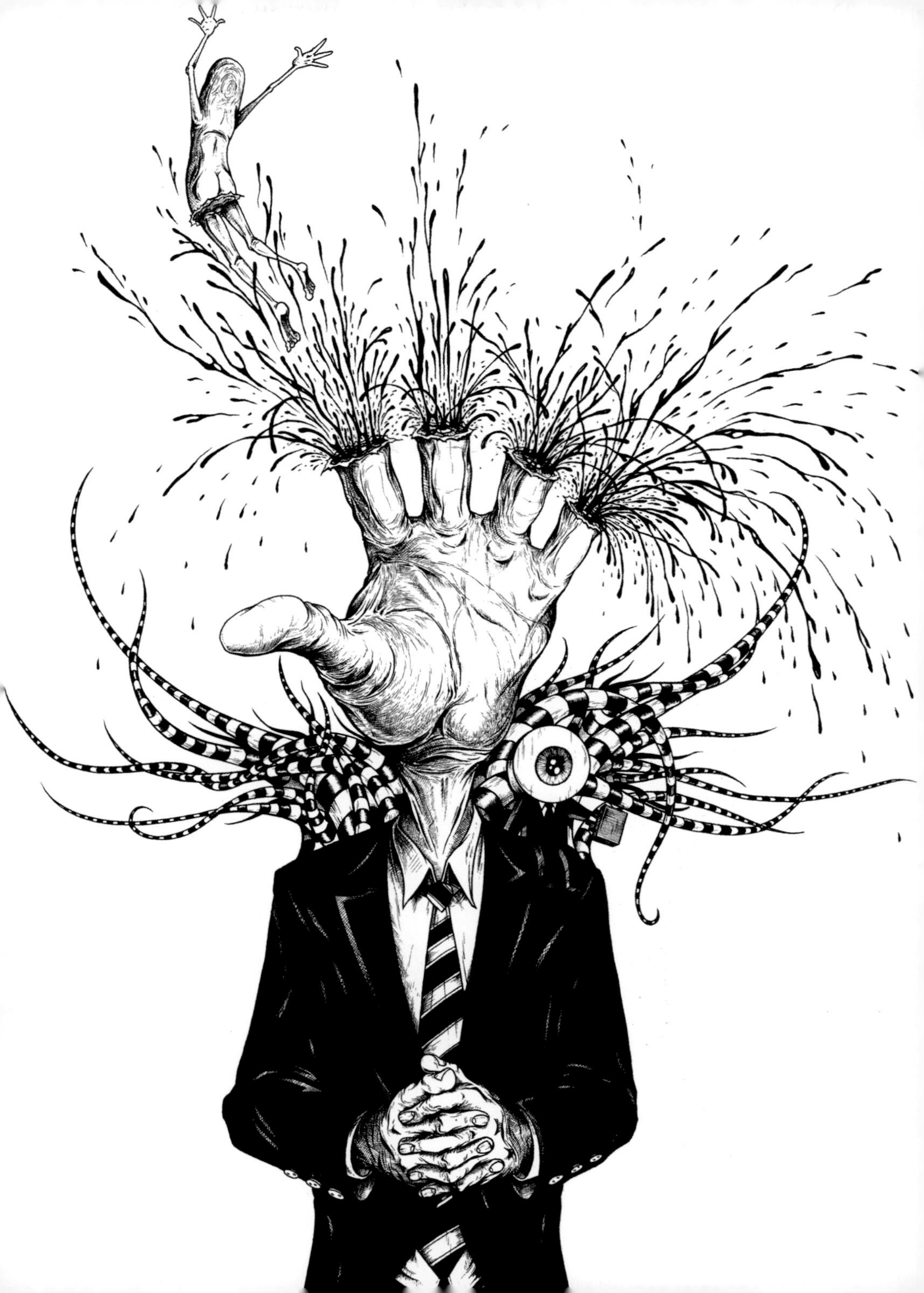

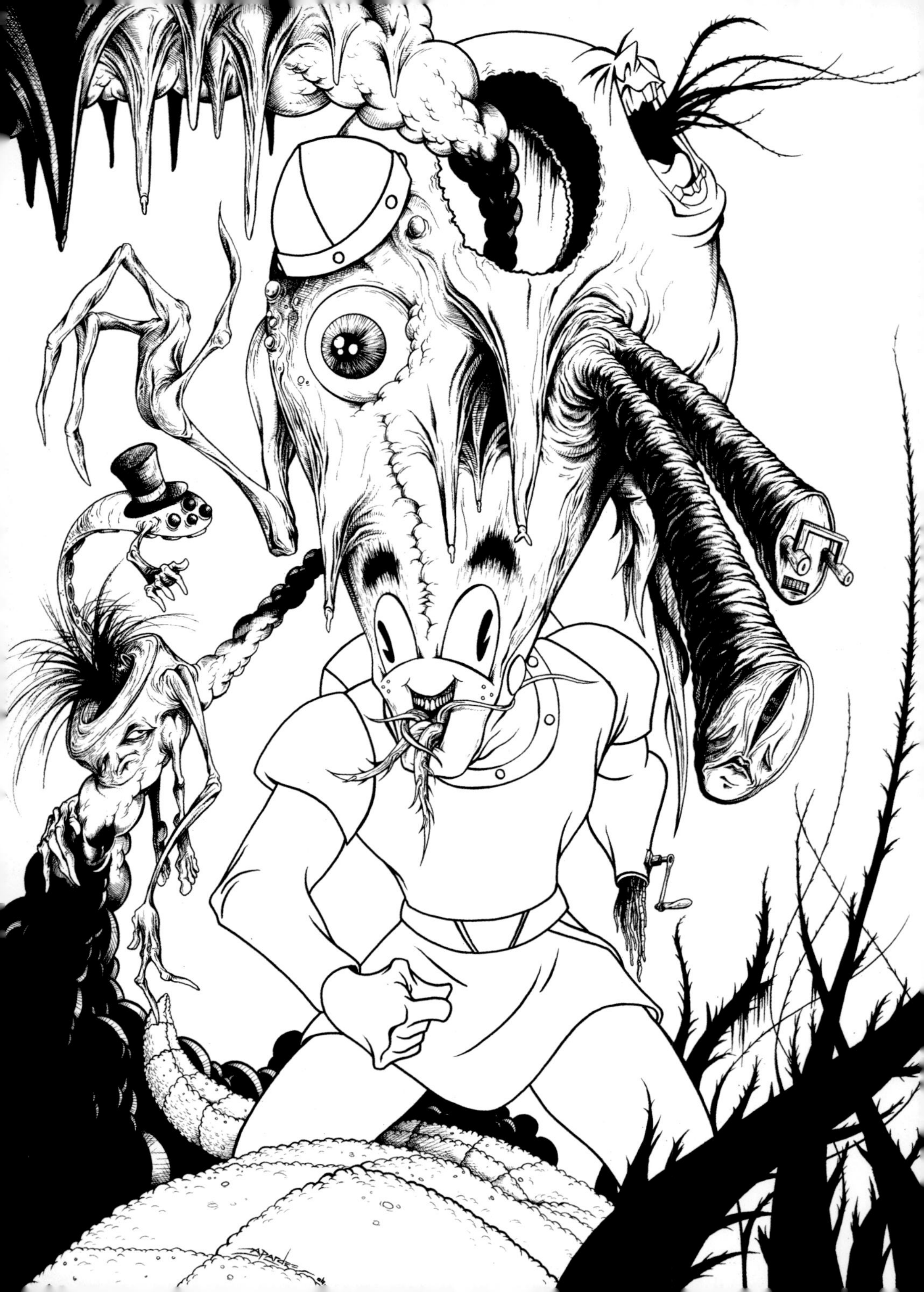

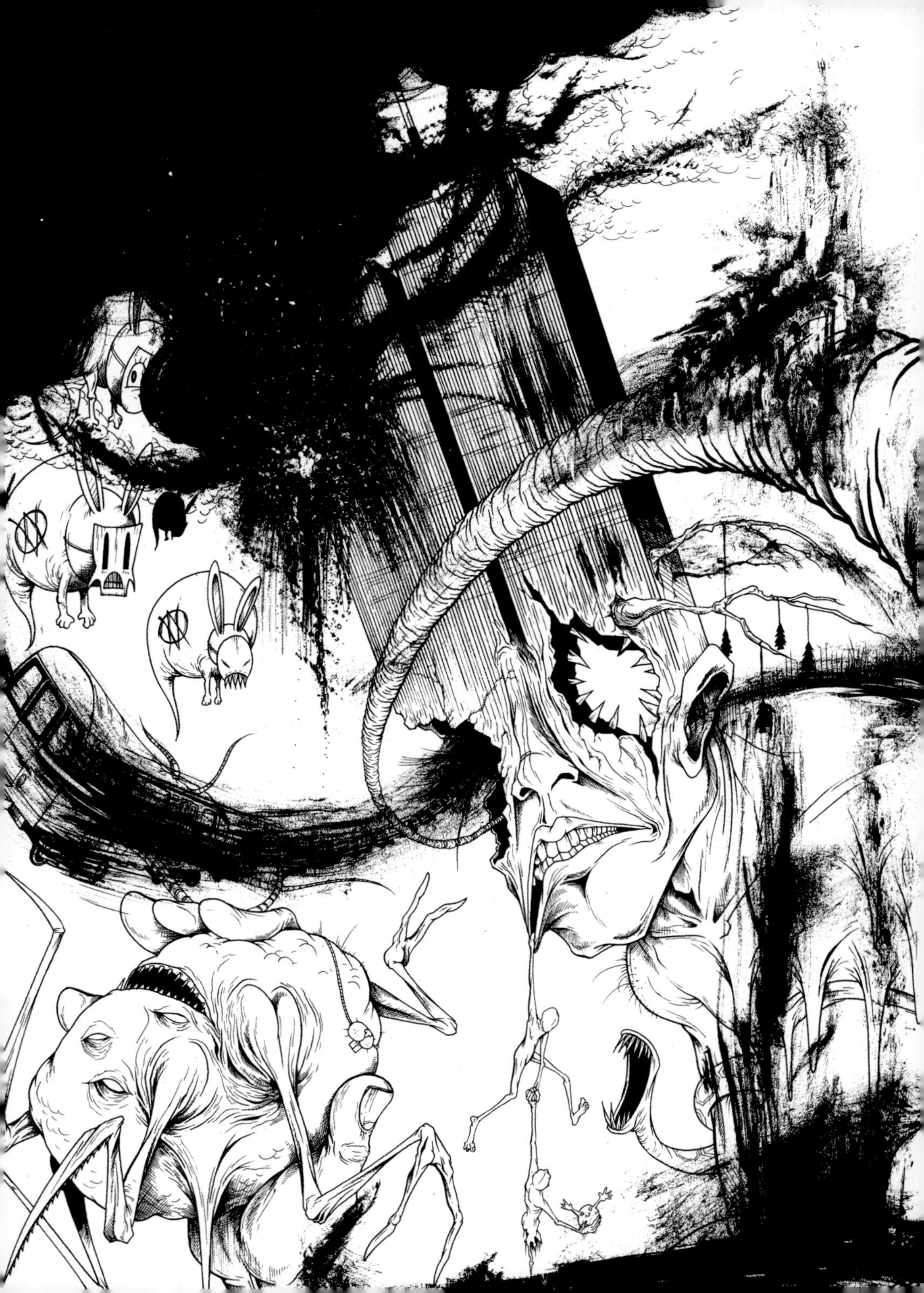

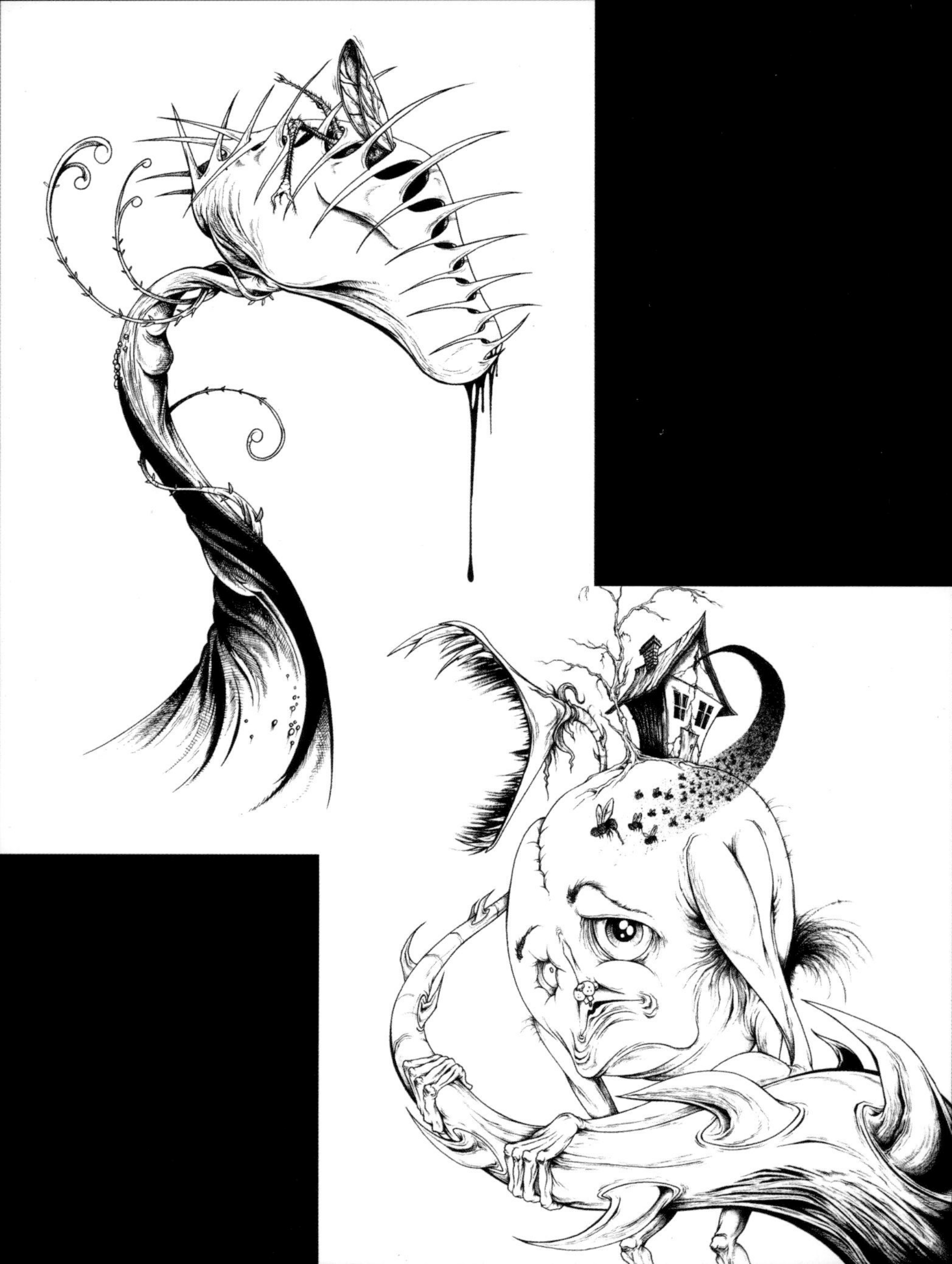

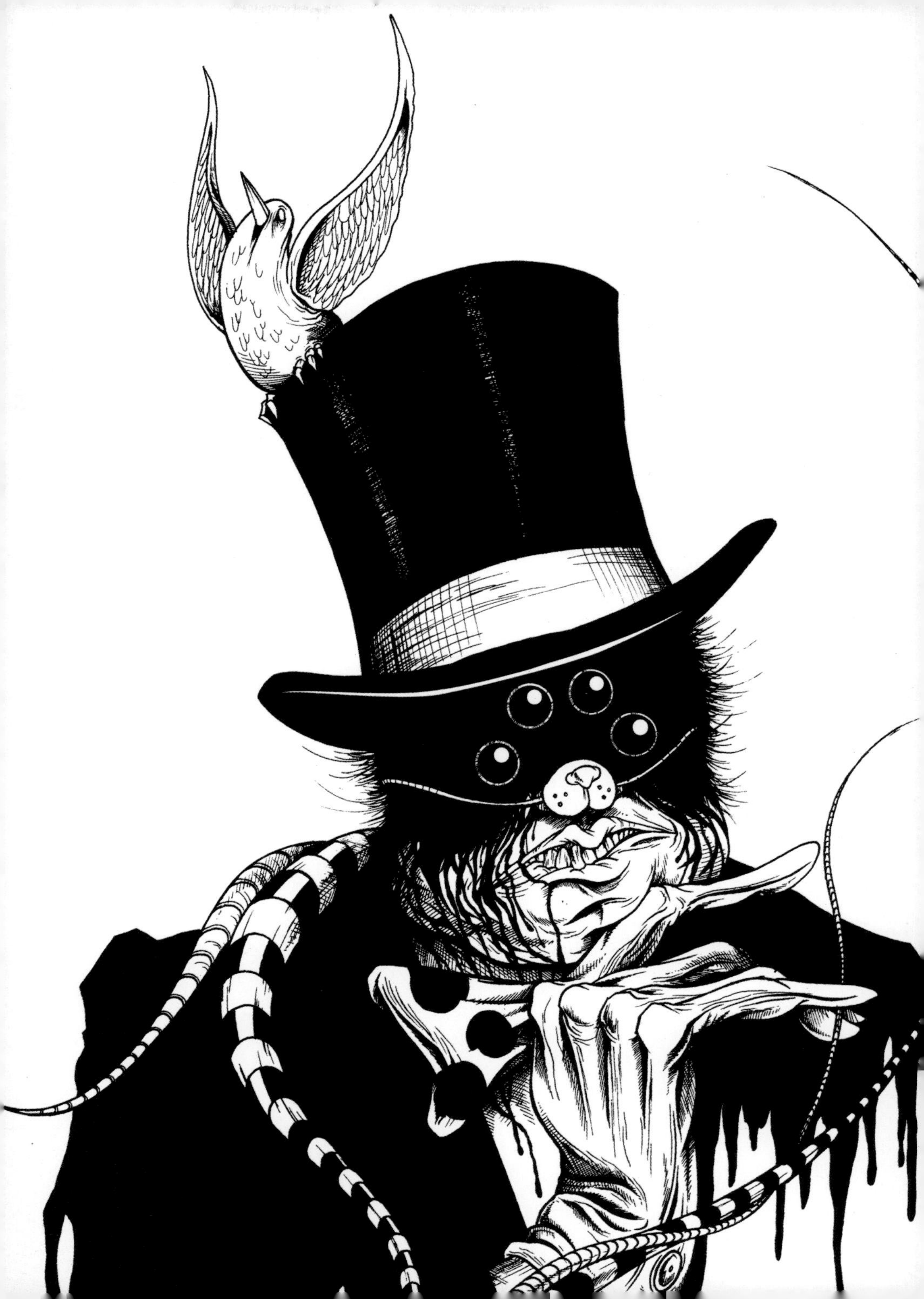

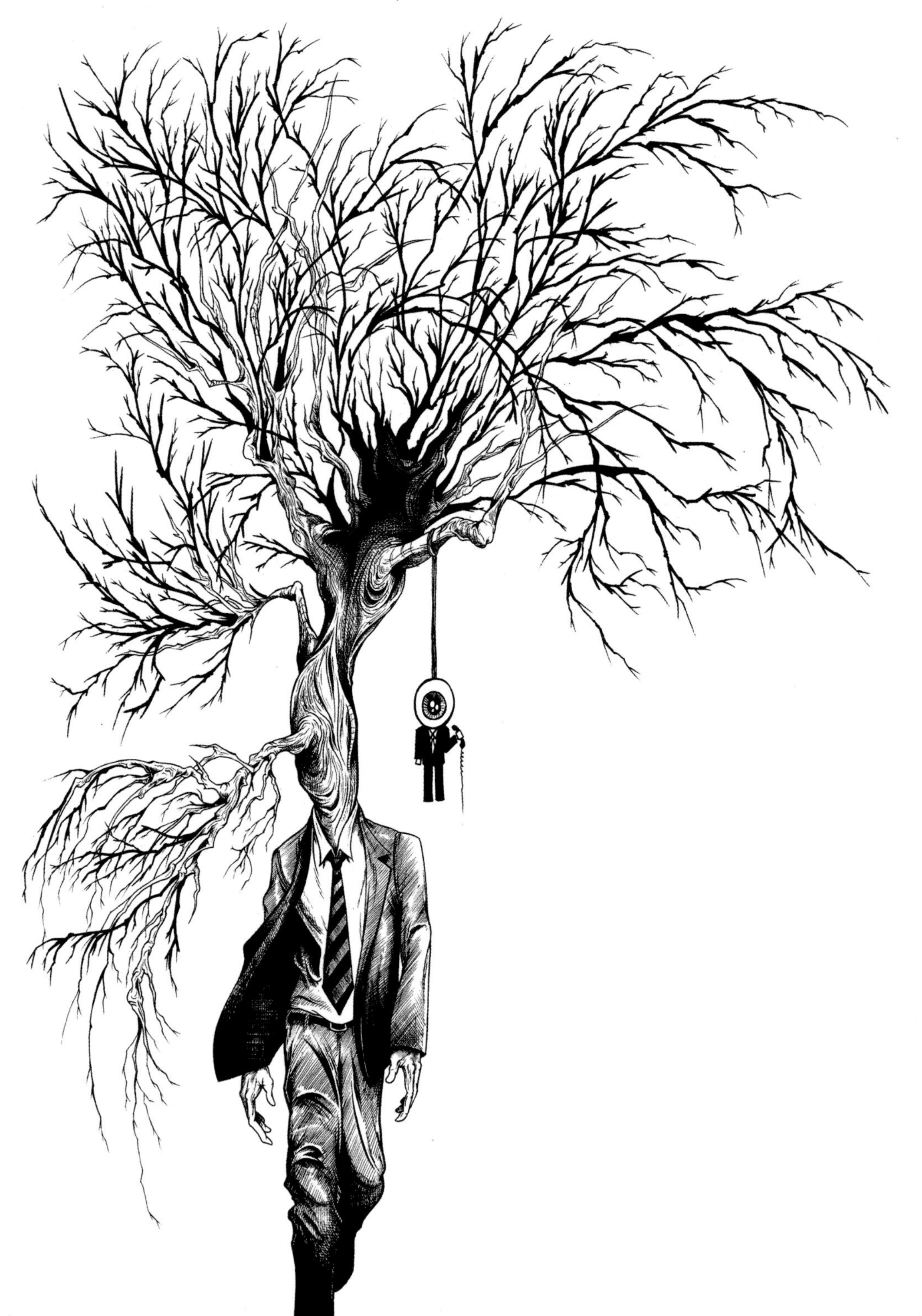

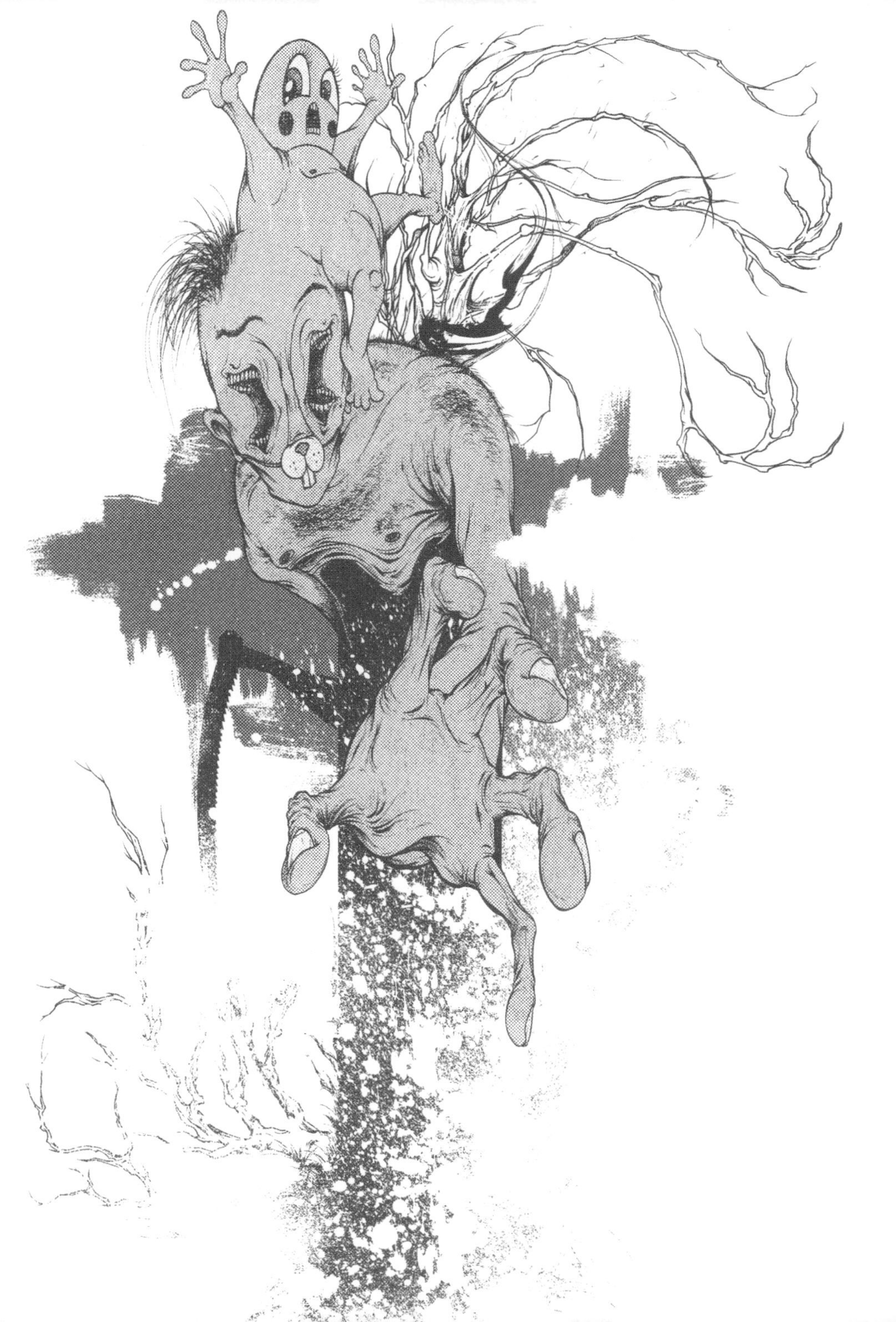

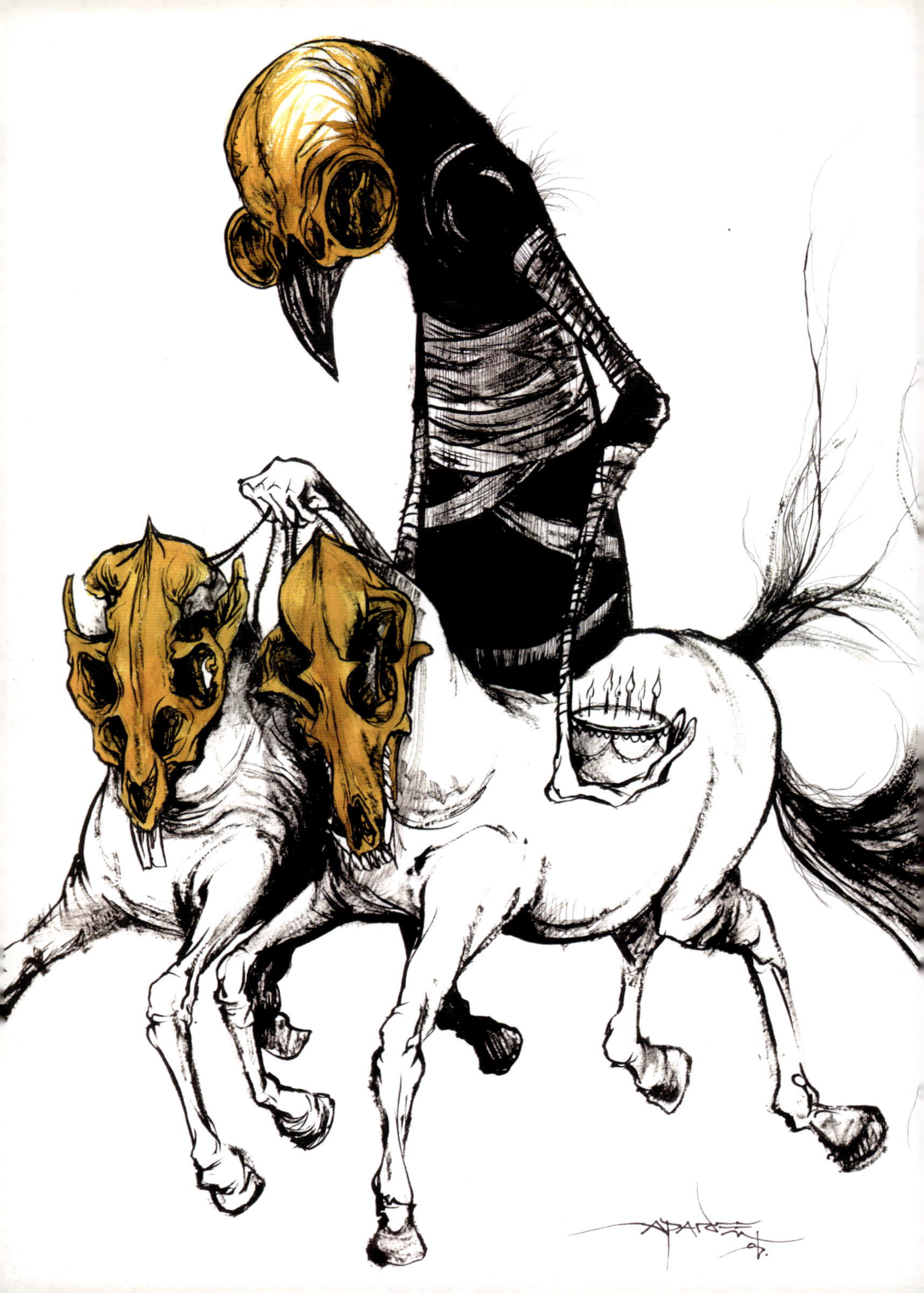

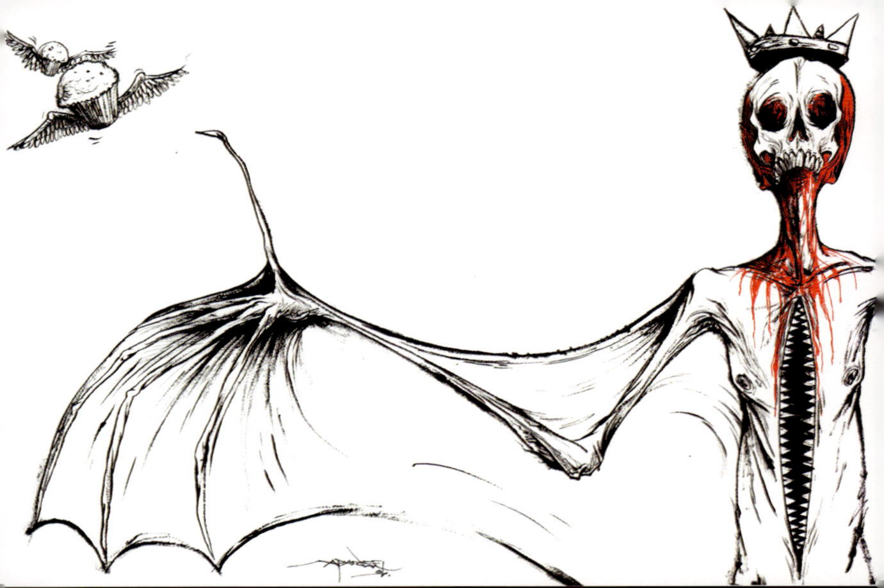

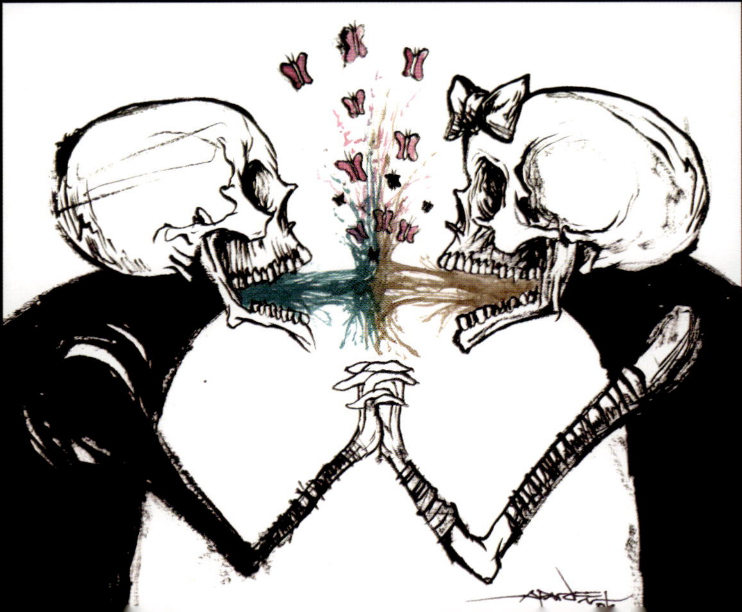

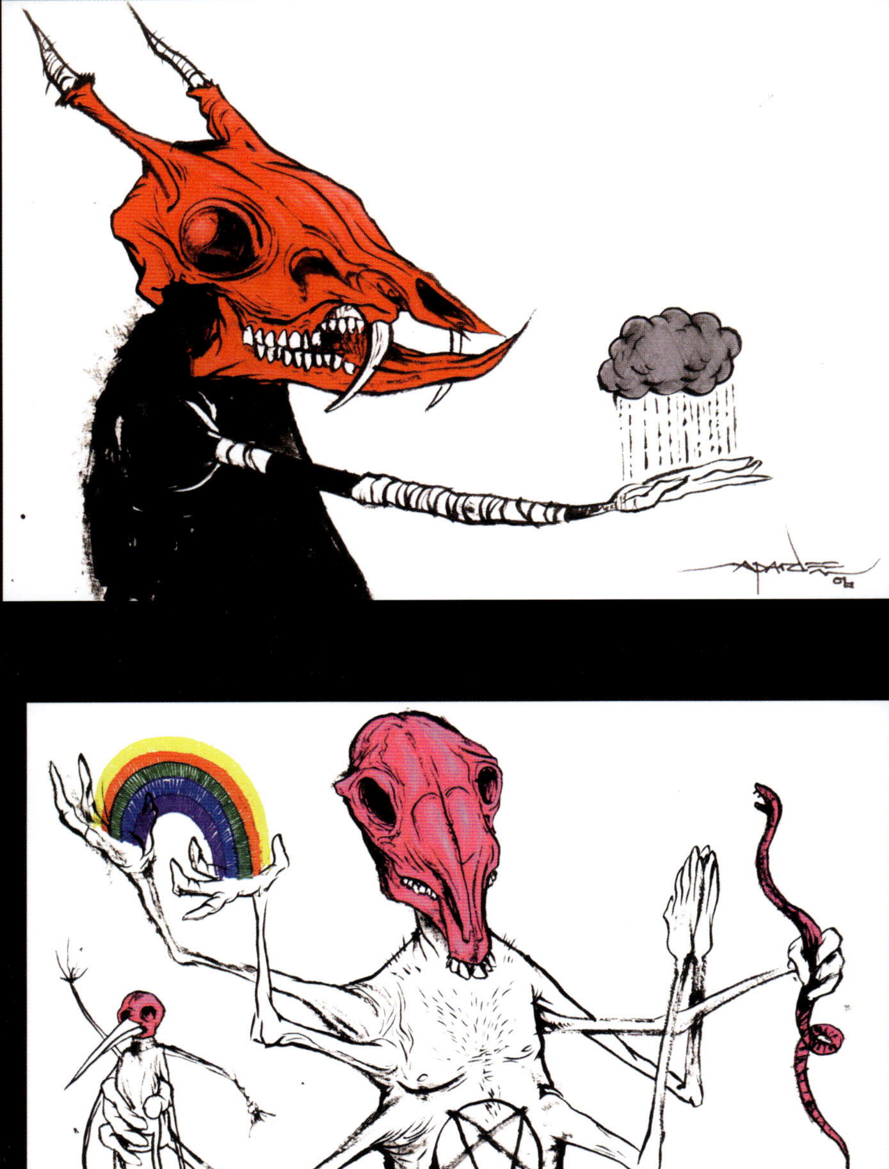

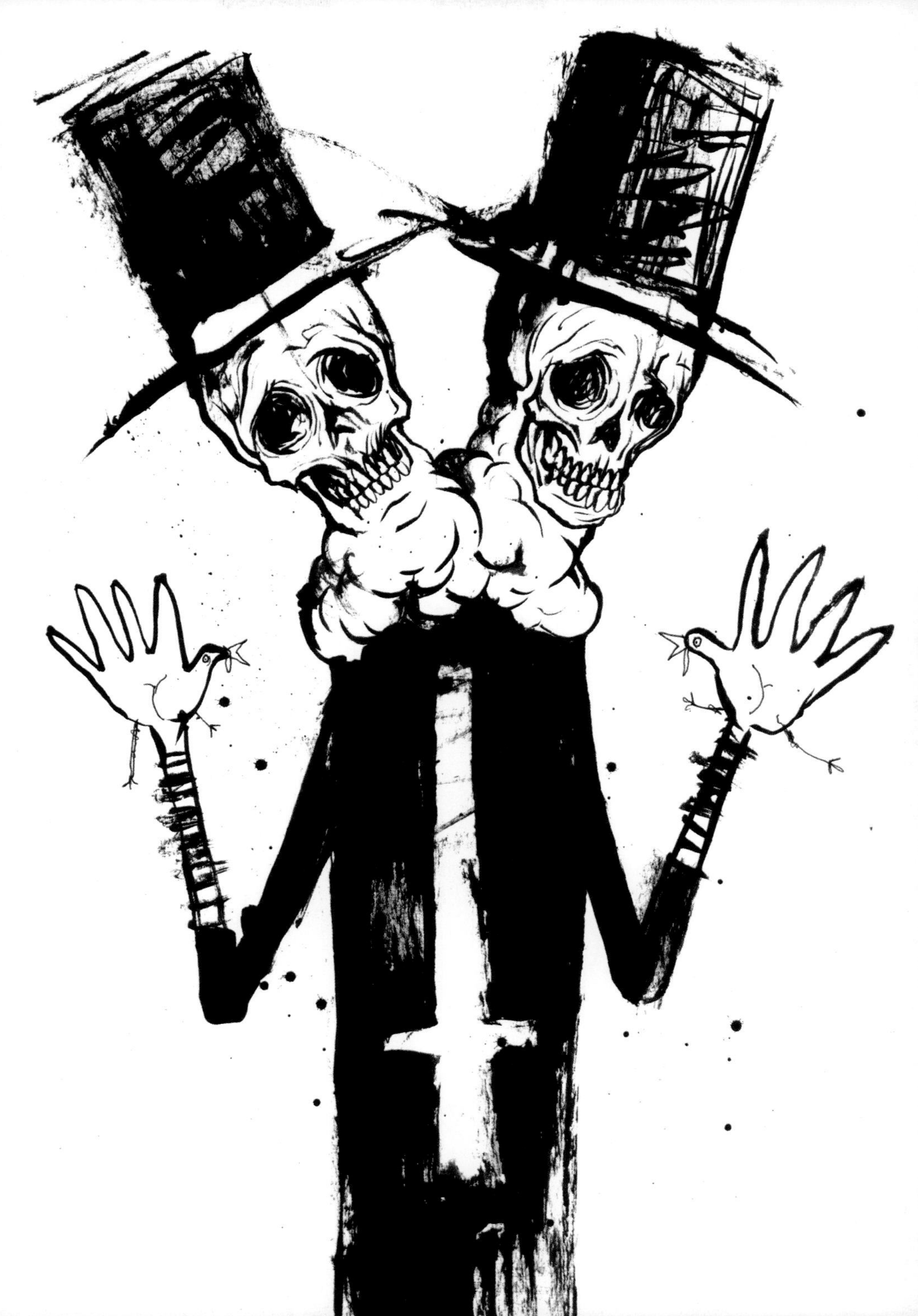

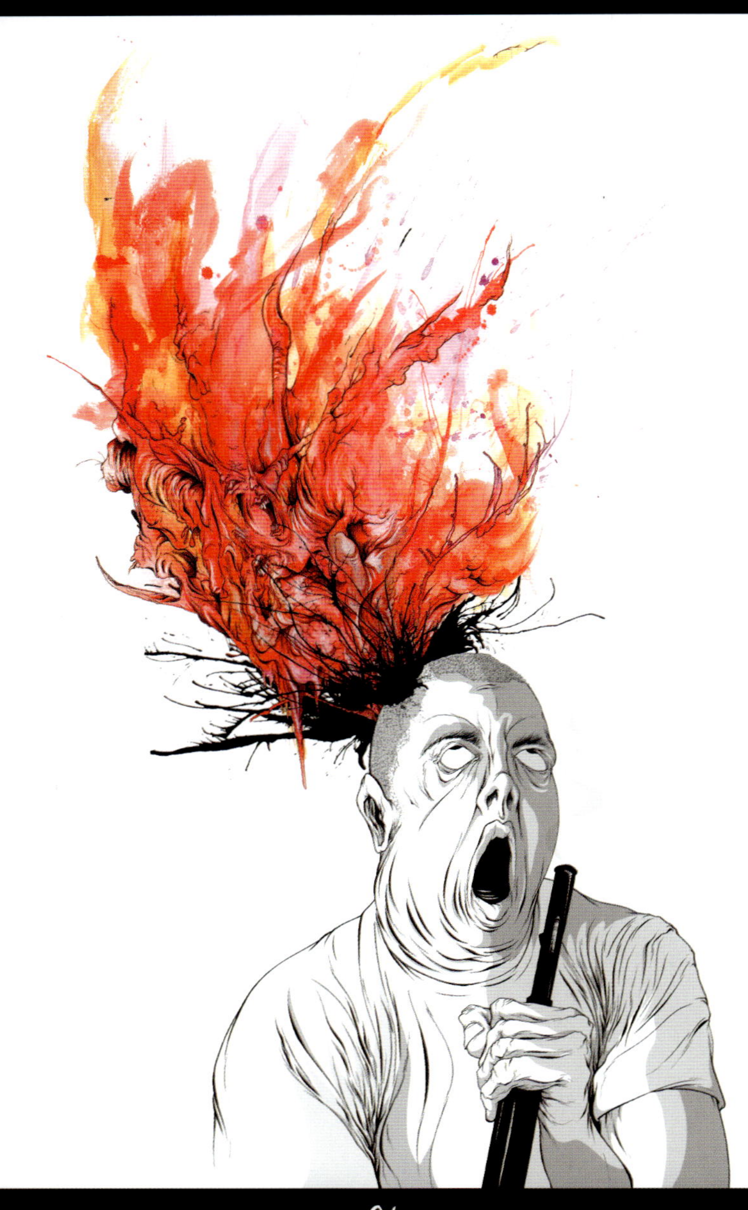

This is my rifle.
There are ~~MANY like it,~~ but this
one is mine.

These 5 things changed my life, and/or influenced my art (in no particular order)

1. Garbage pail kids
2. Street Fighter II
3. Sam Kieth
4. Graffiti
5. Going to the mental institution and being on medication for 15 years.

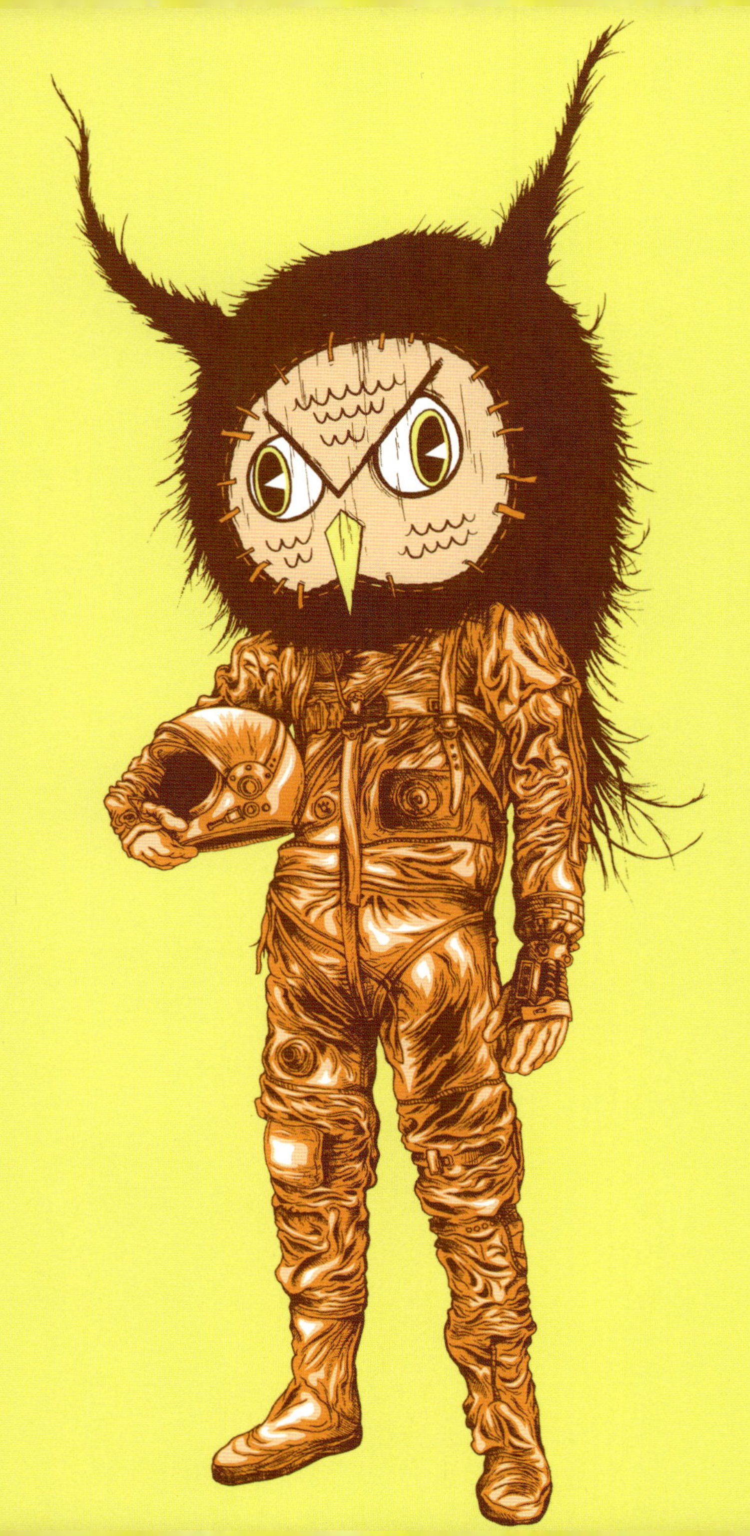

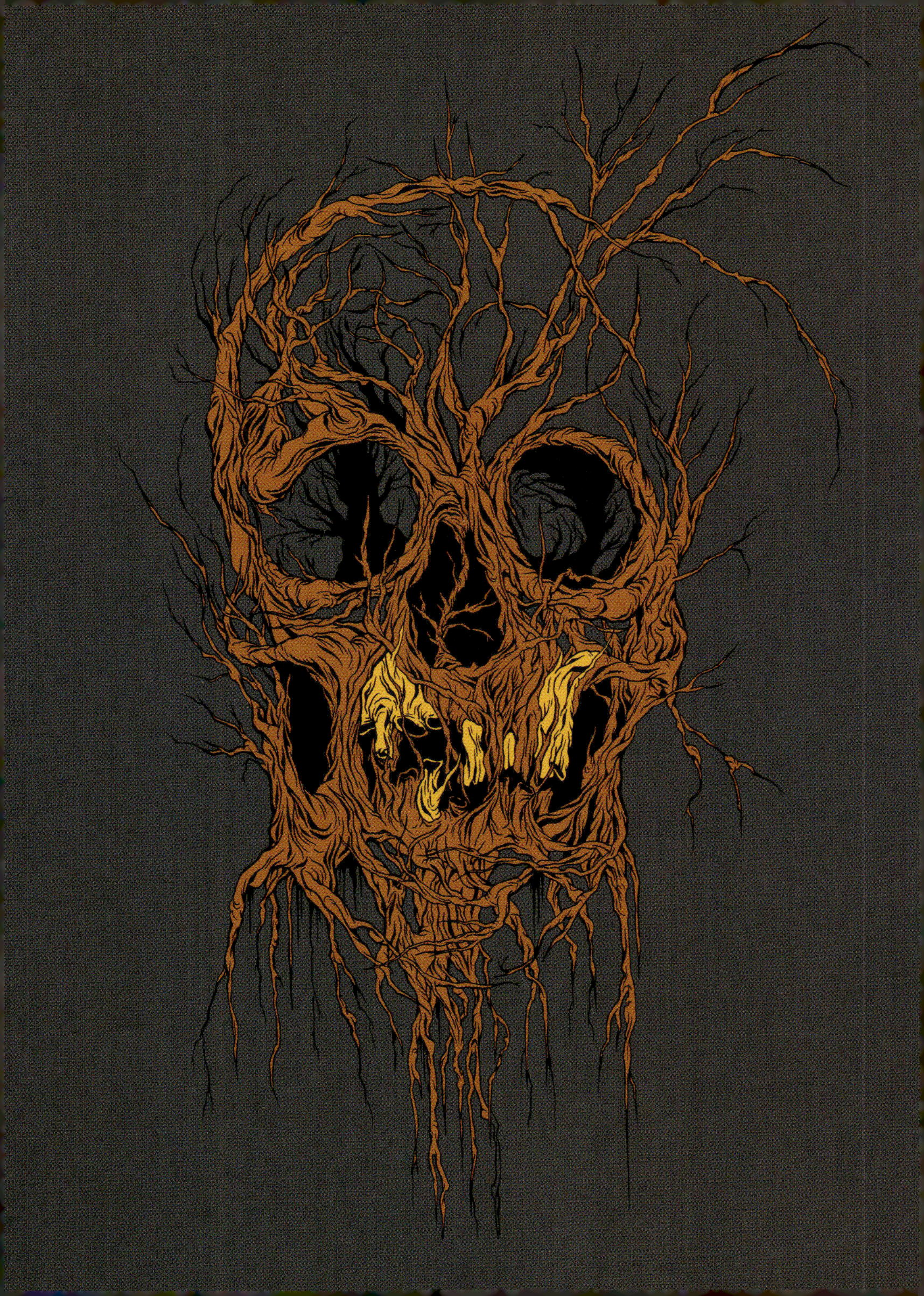

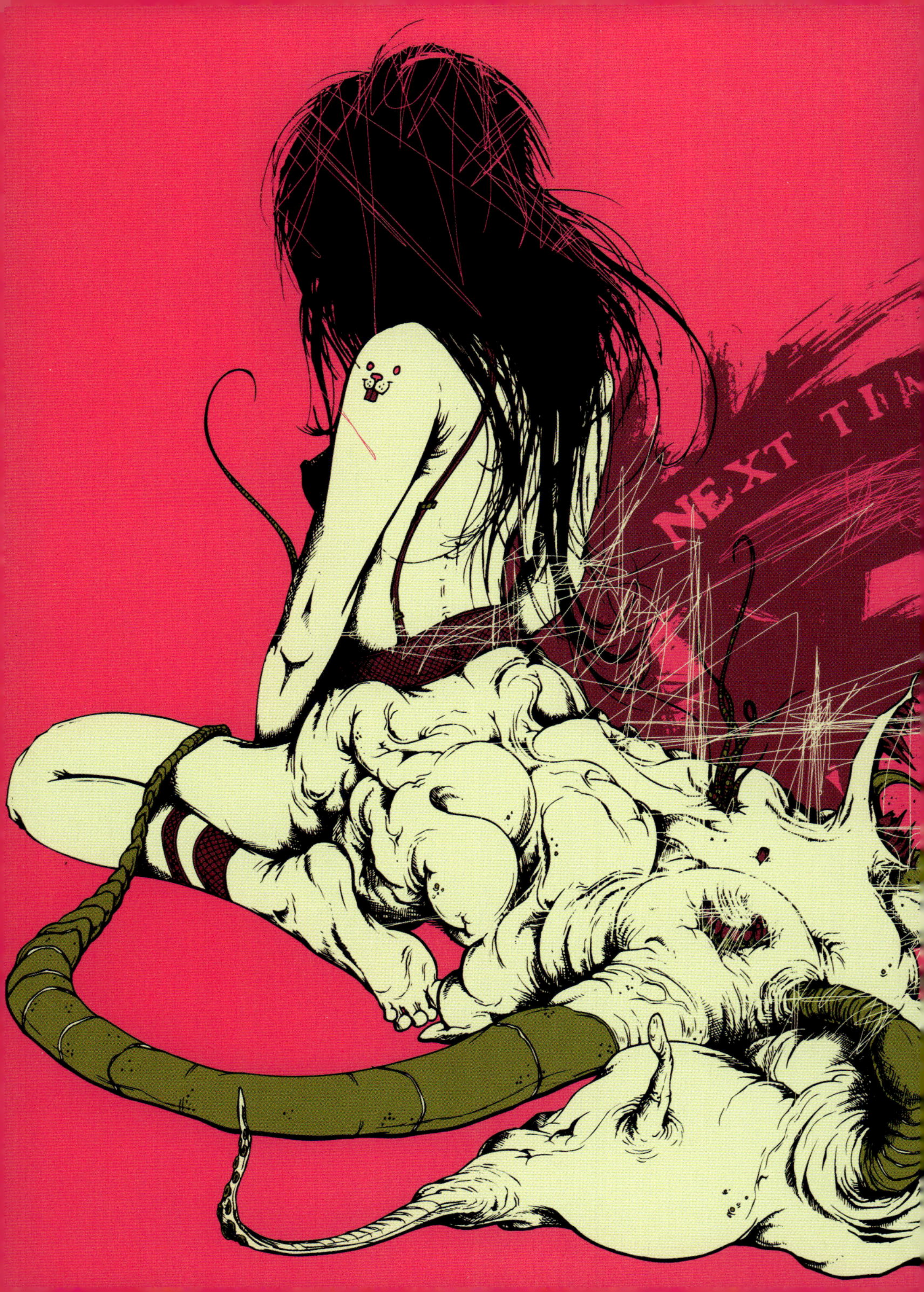
NEXT TI

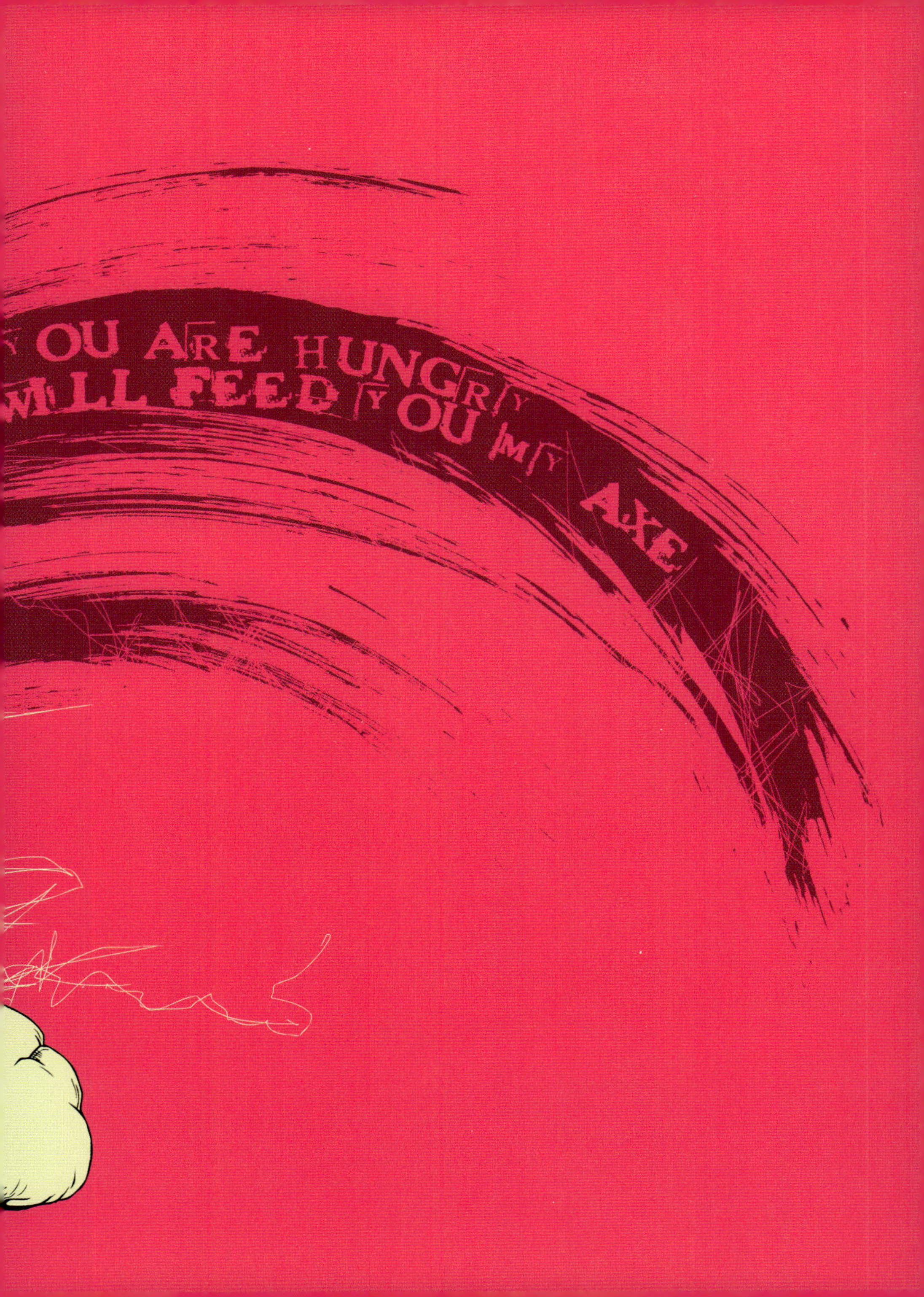

YOU ARE HUNGRY
WILL FEED YOU MY AXE

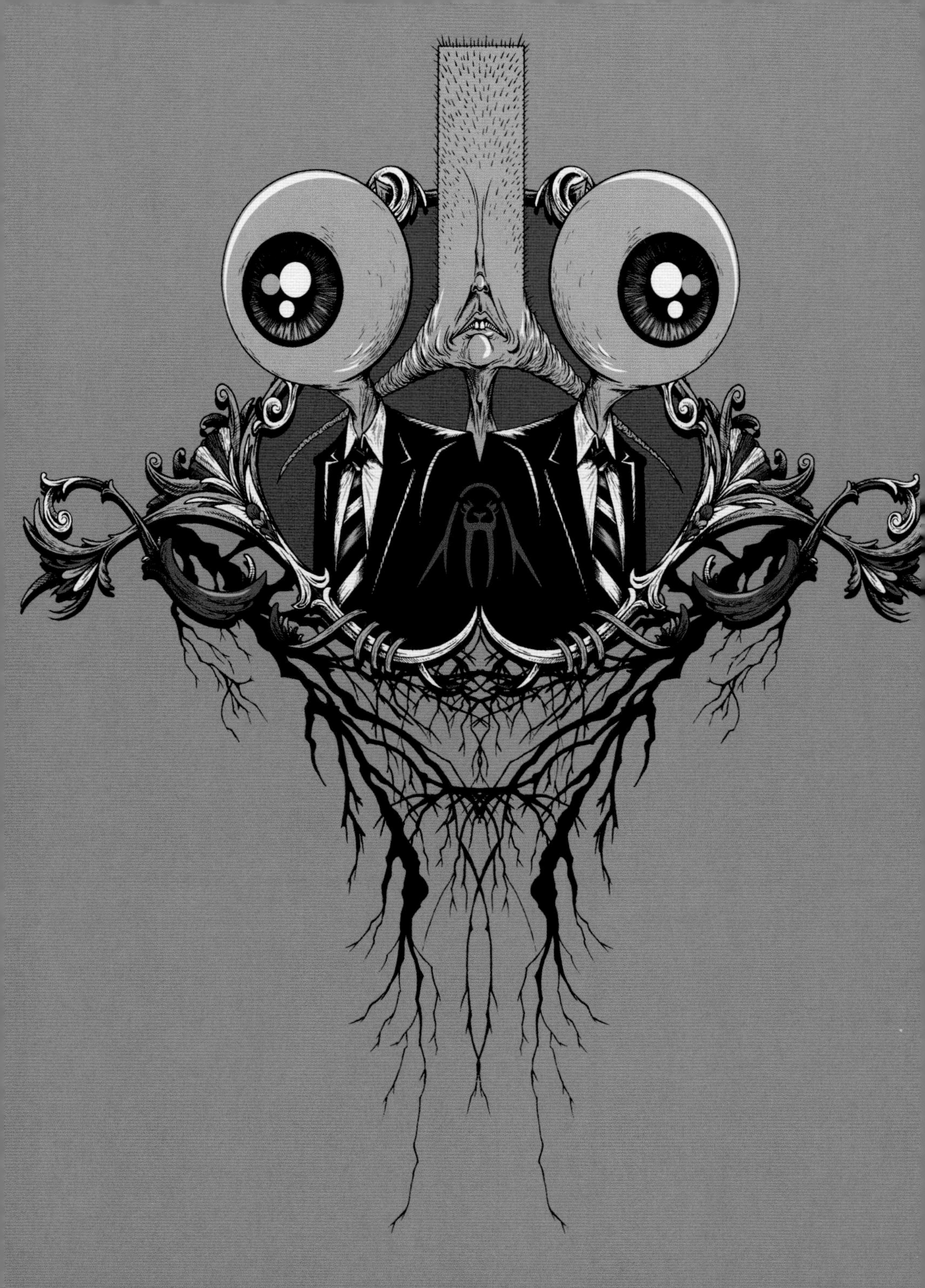

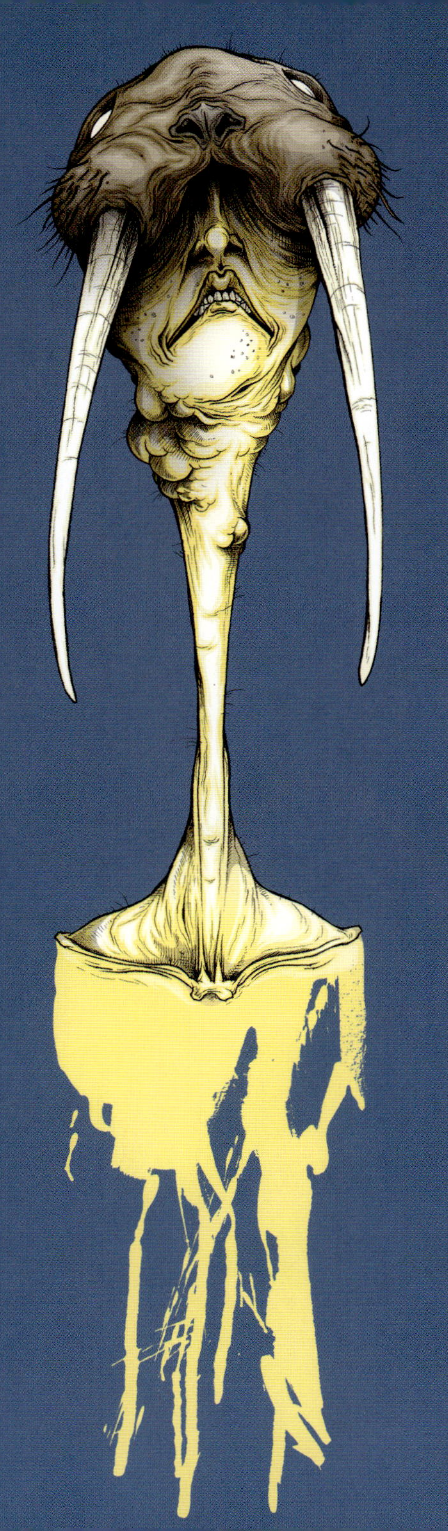

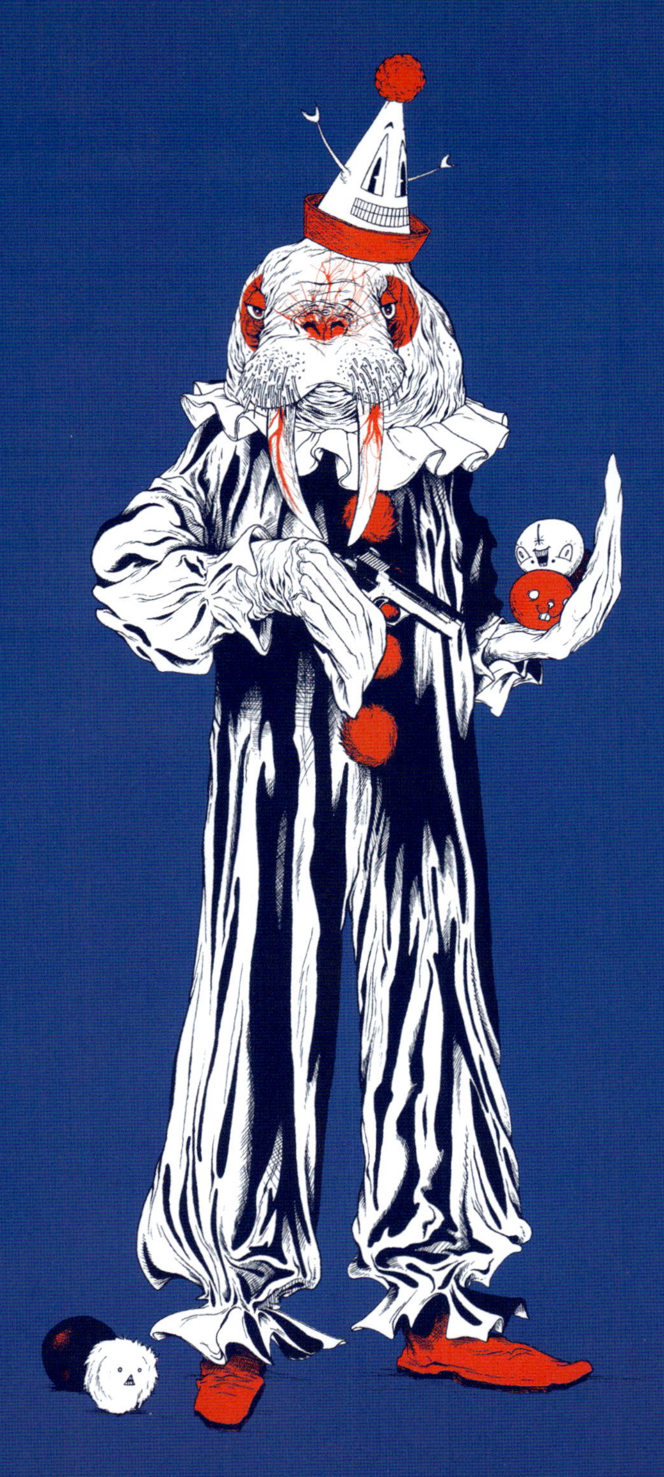

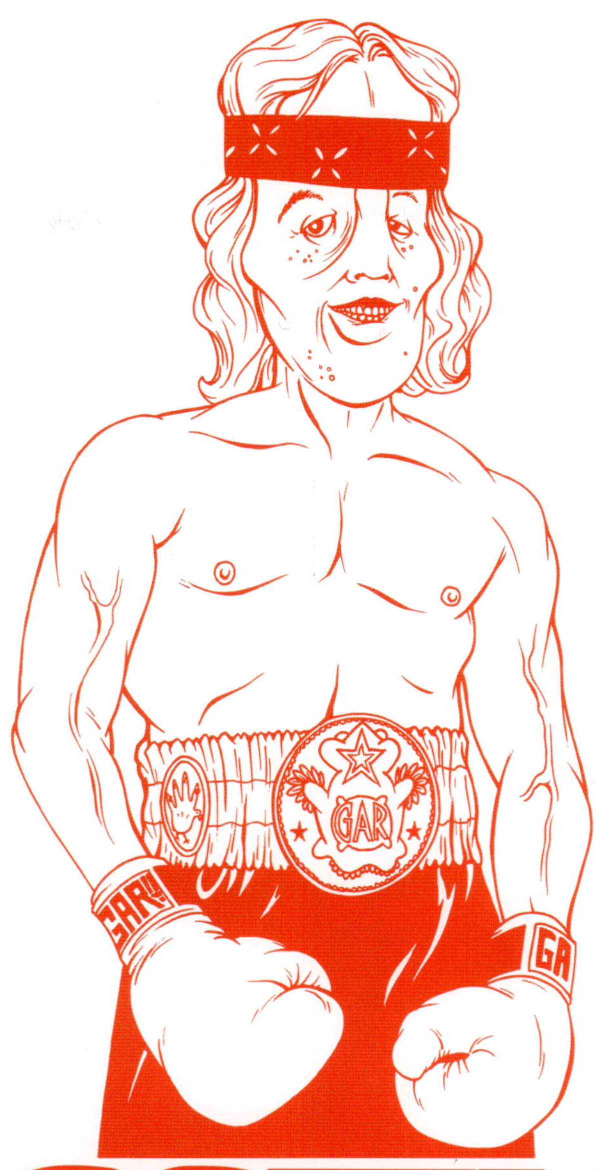

ROCKY VI

THESE THINGS ARE GOOD

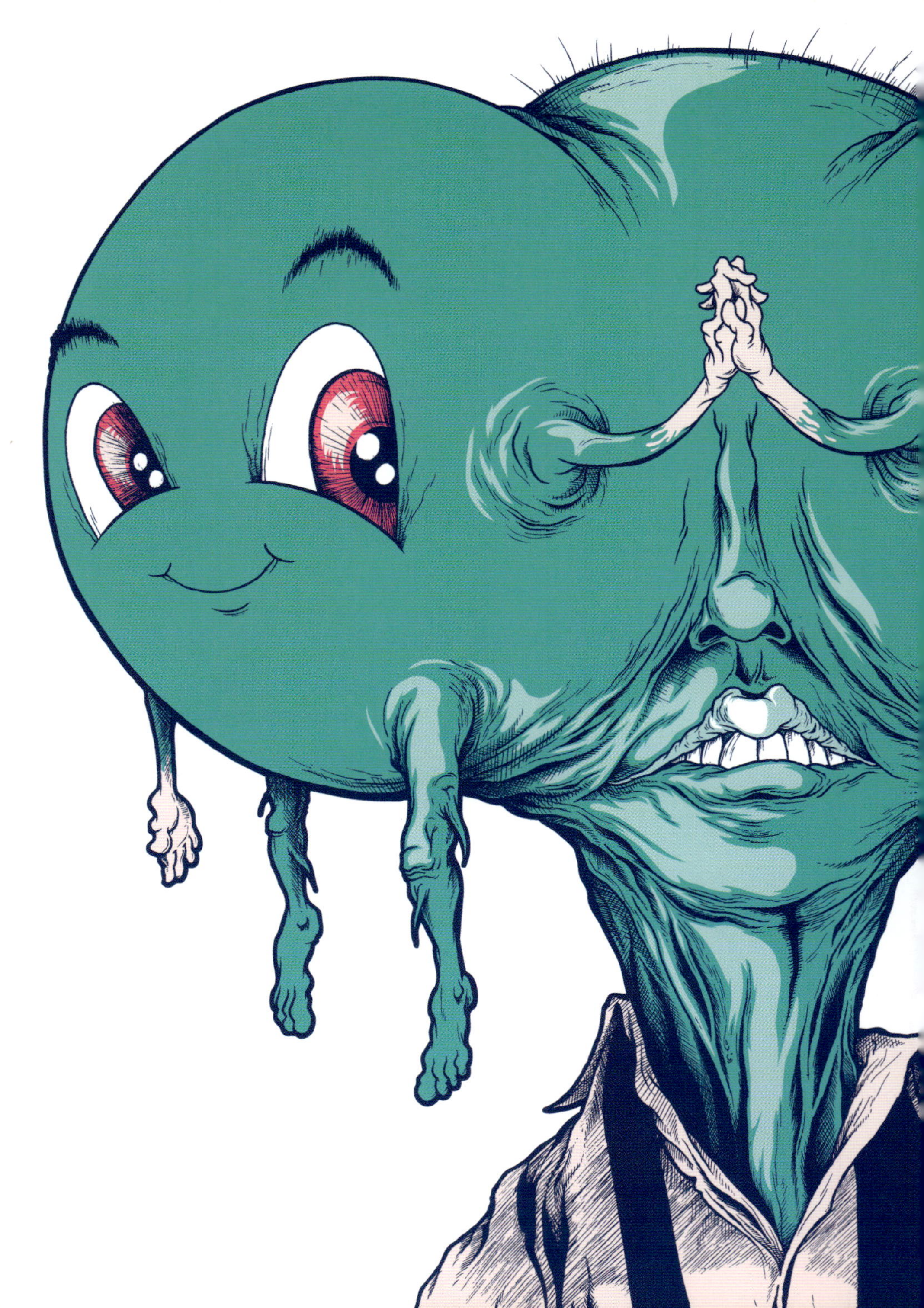

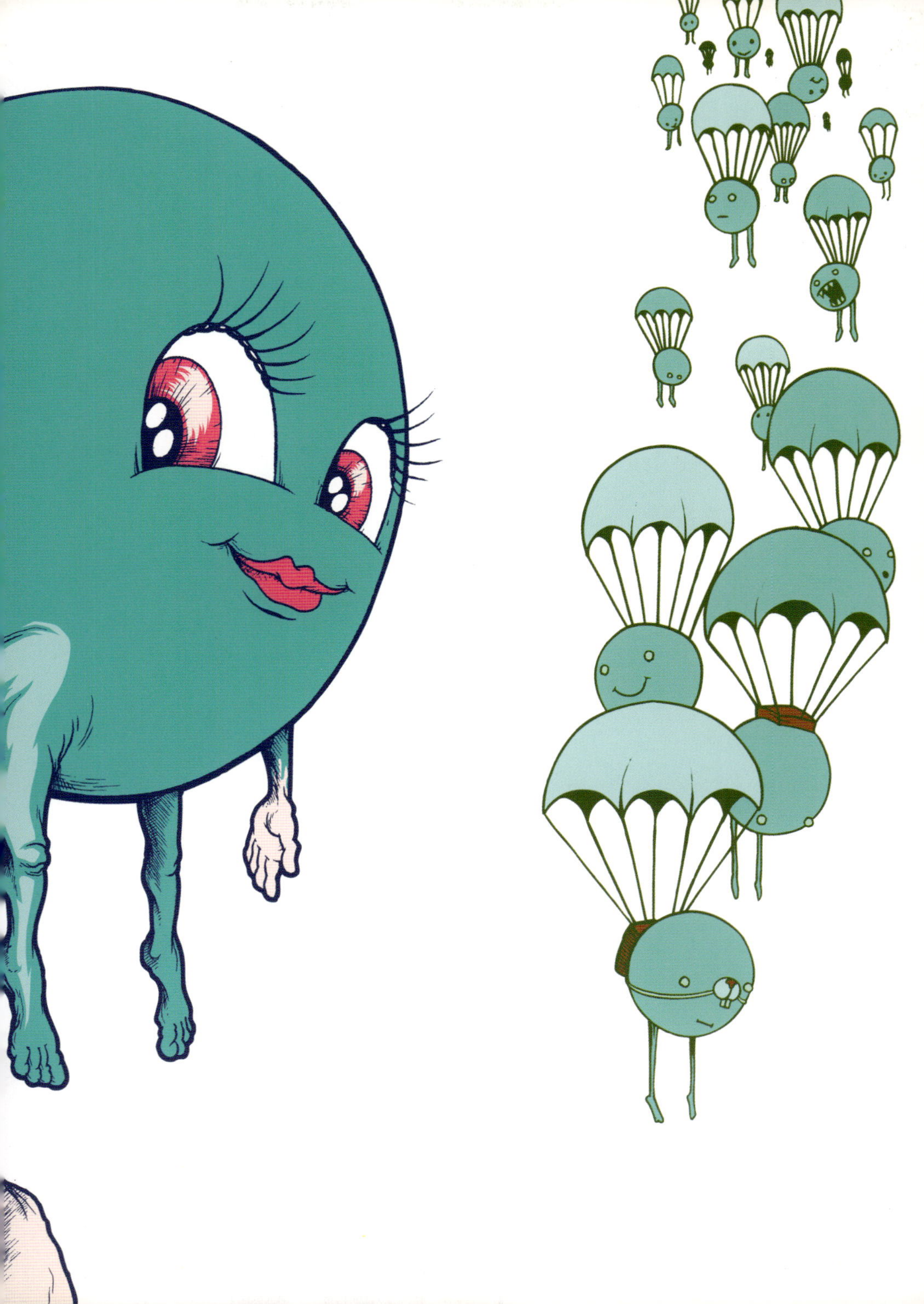

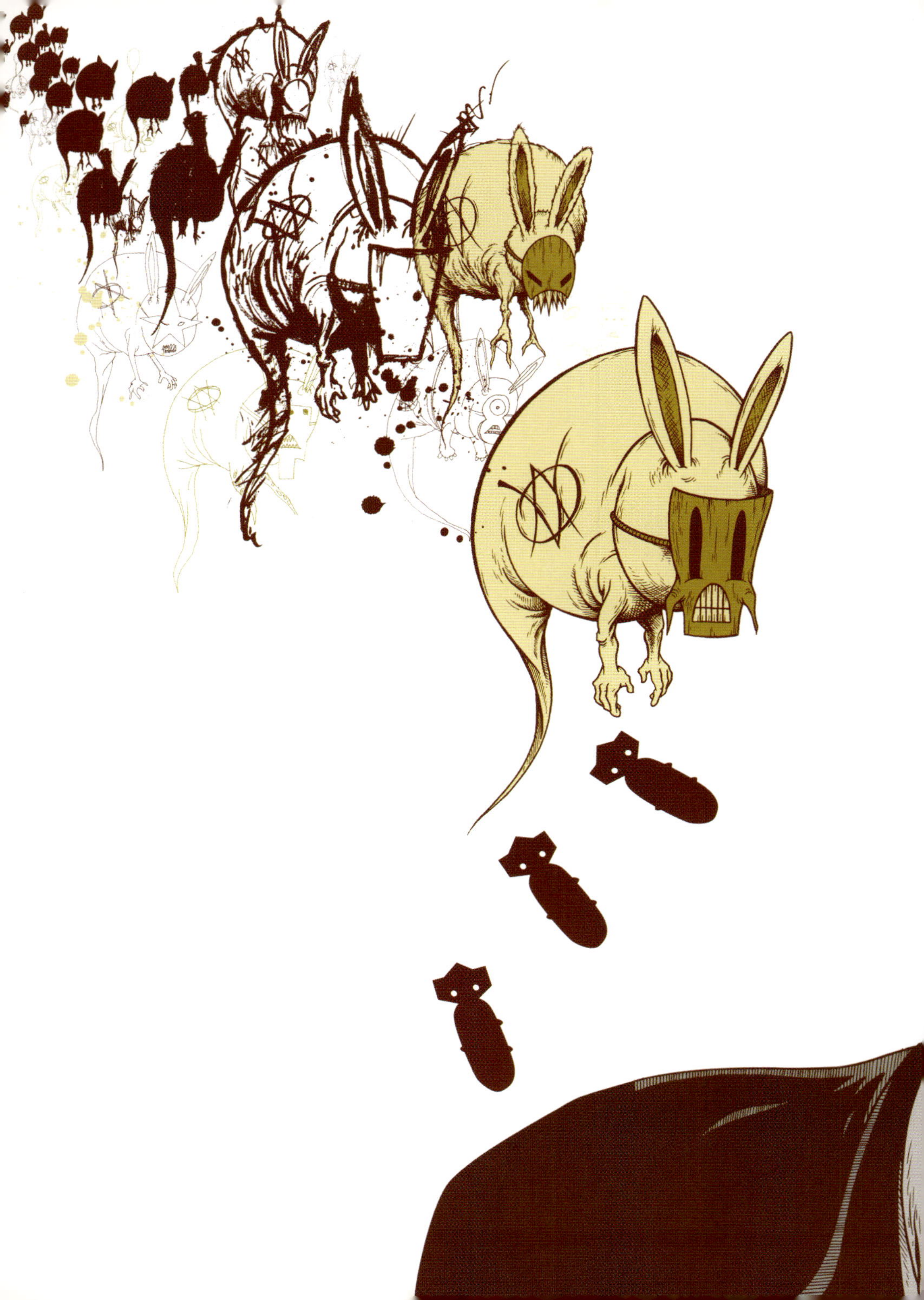

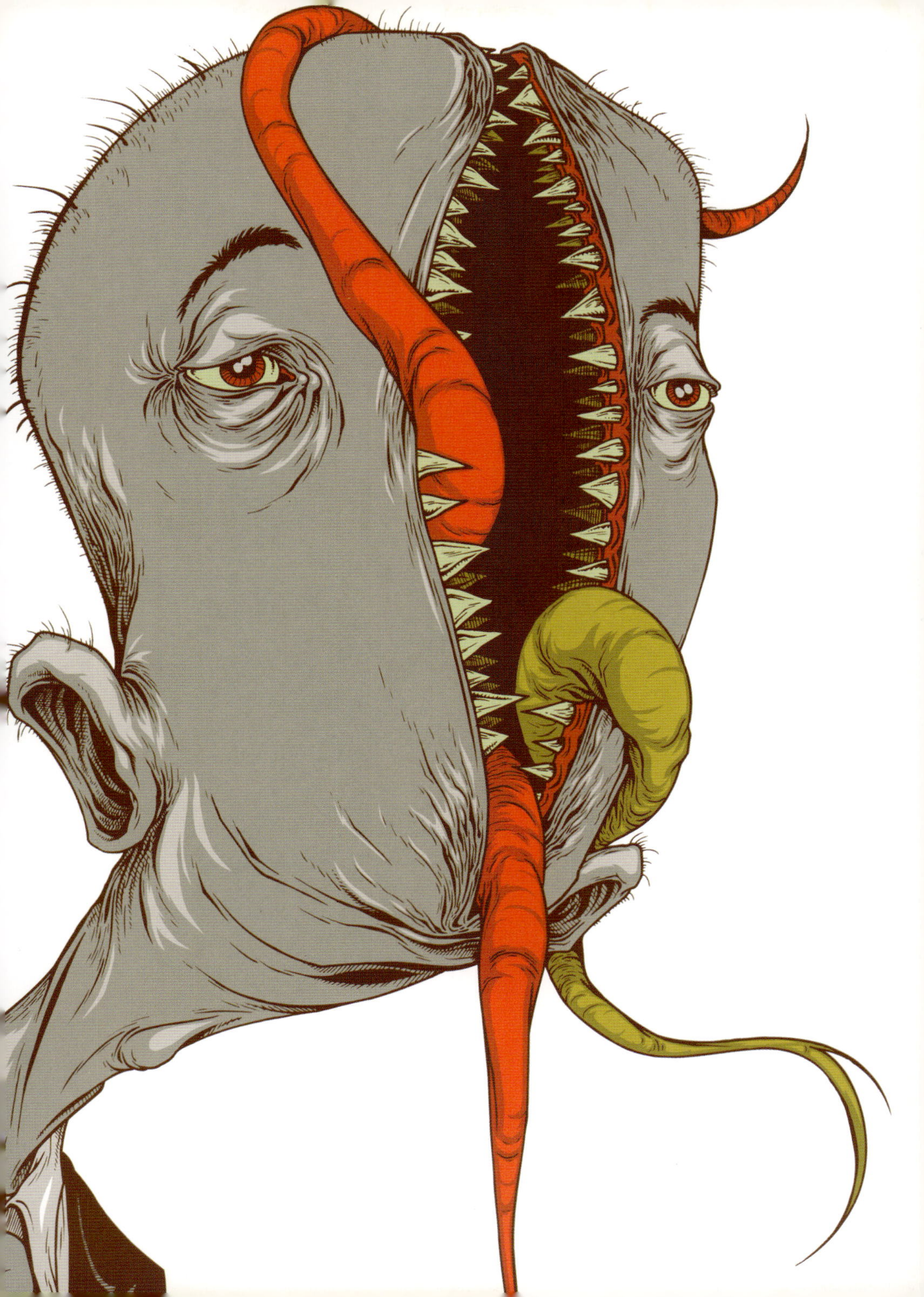

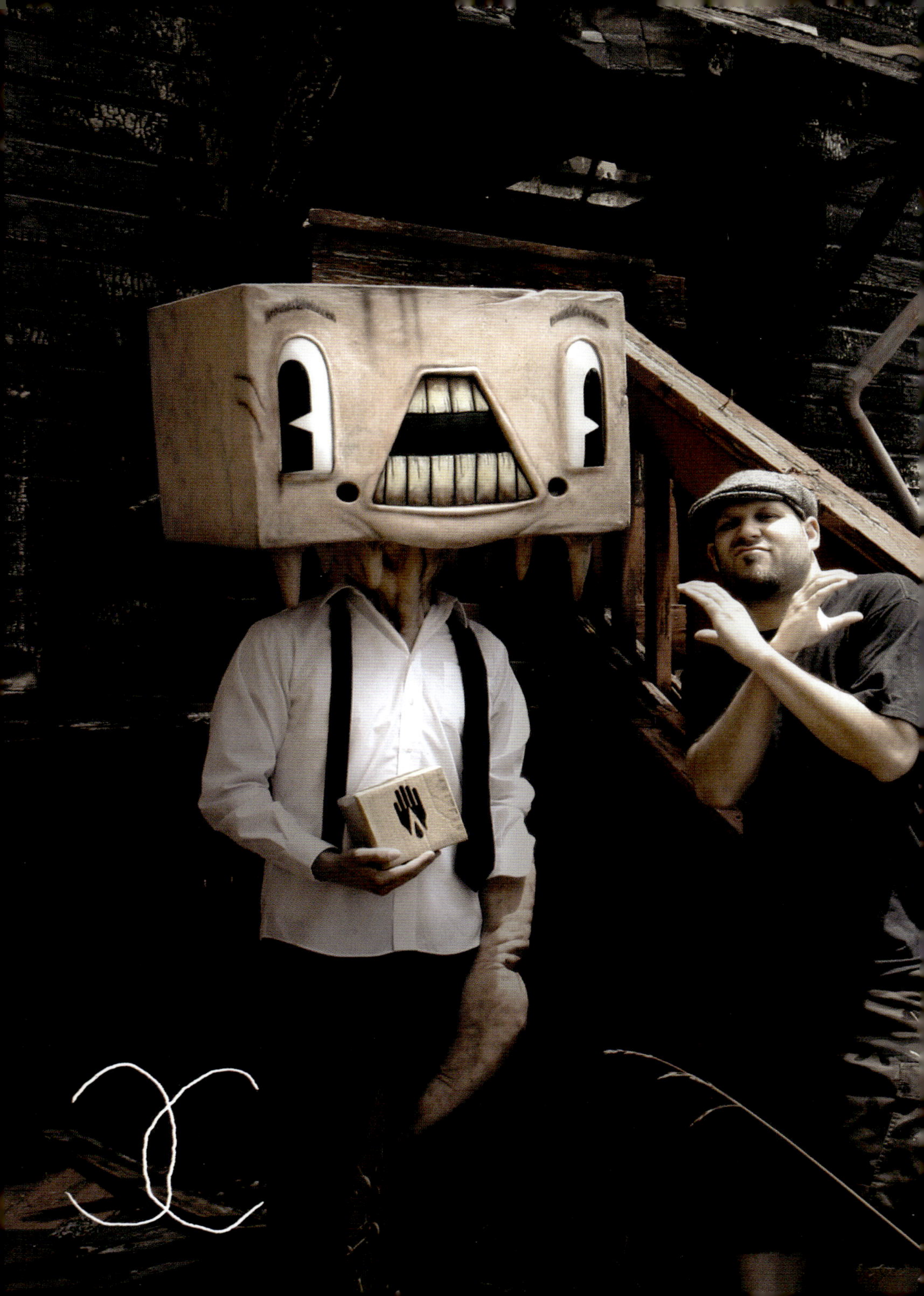

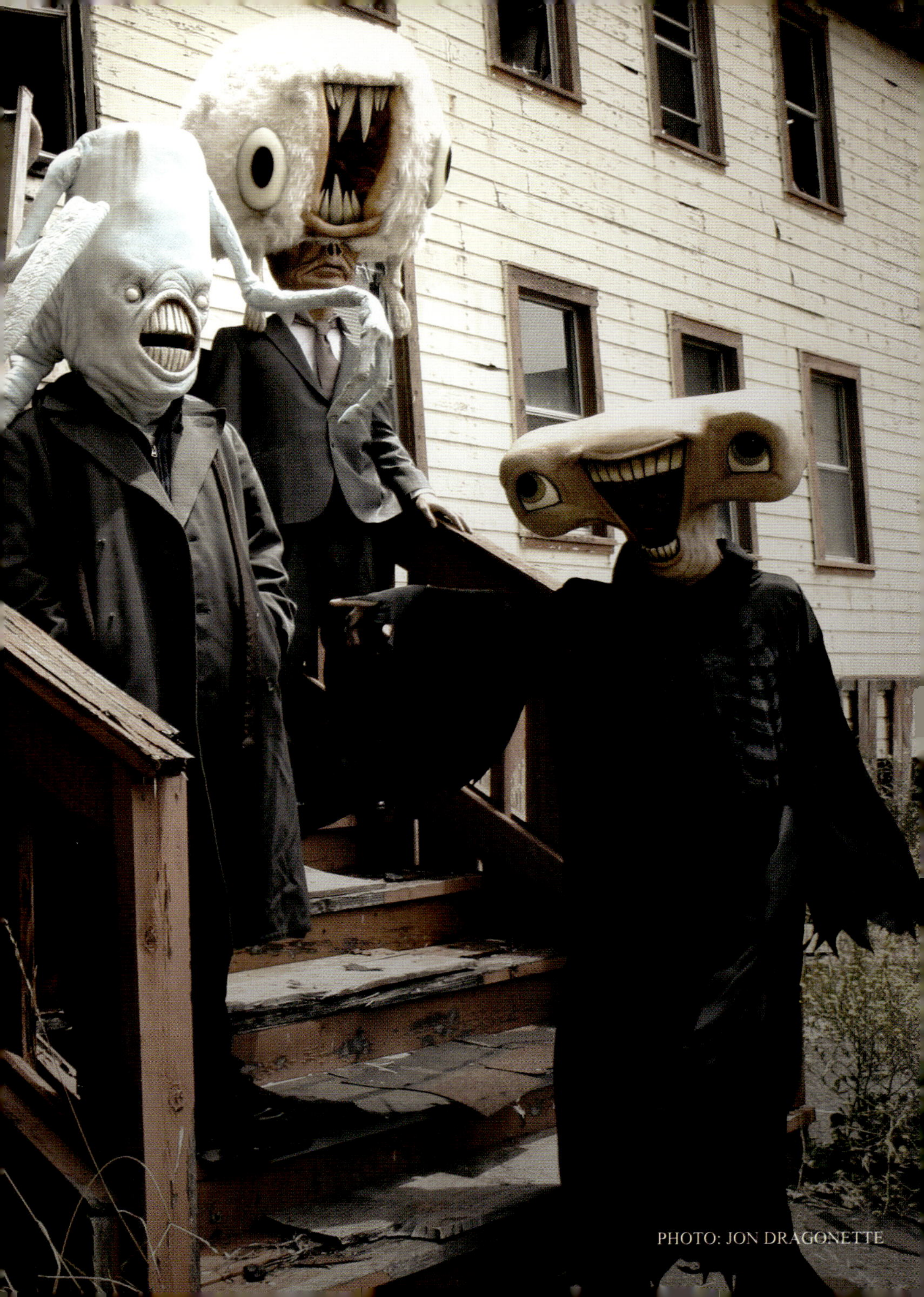

PHOTO: JON DRAGONETTE

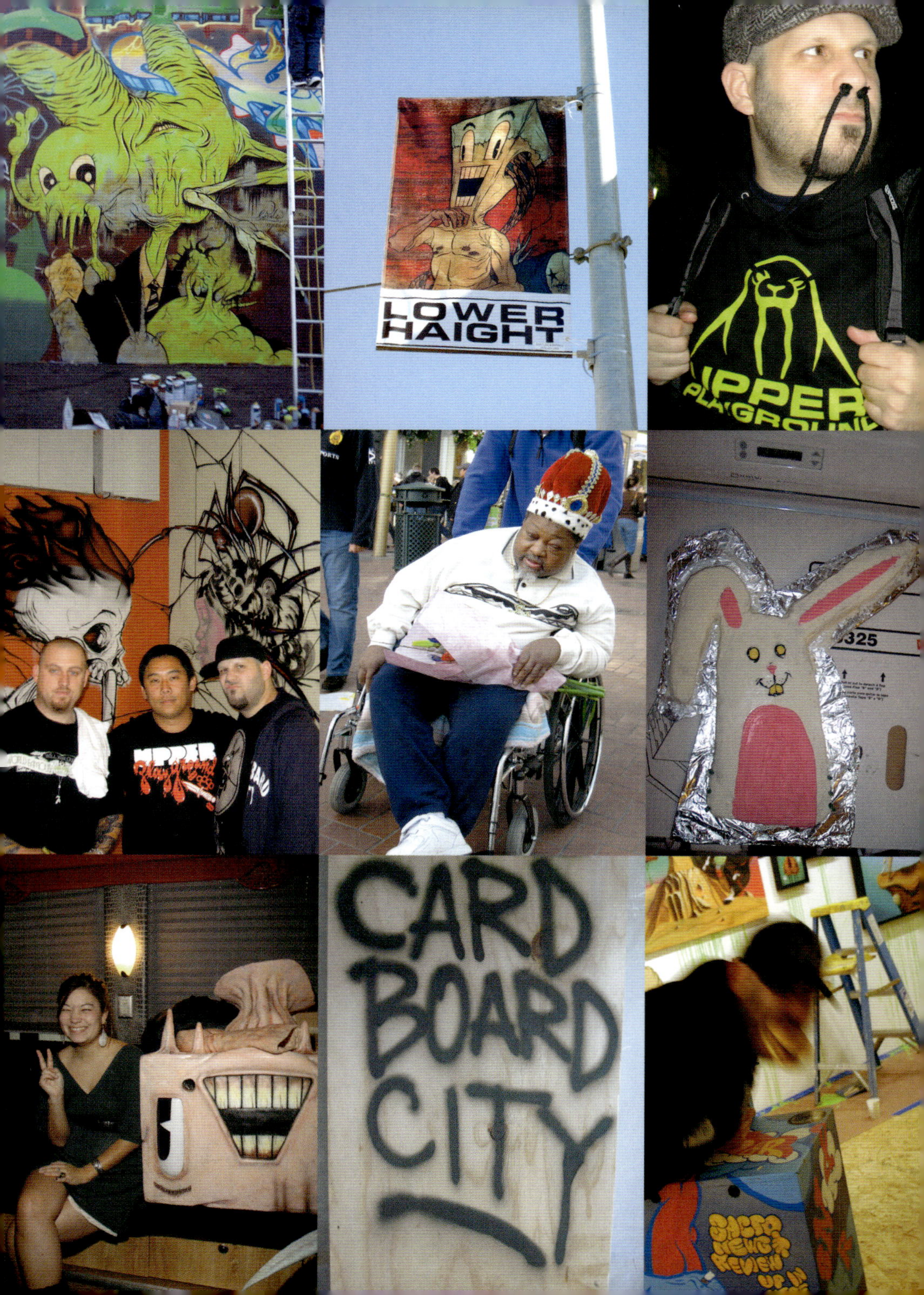

LOWER
HAIGHT
CARD
BOARD
CITY

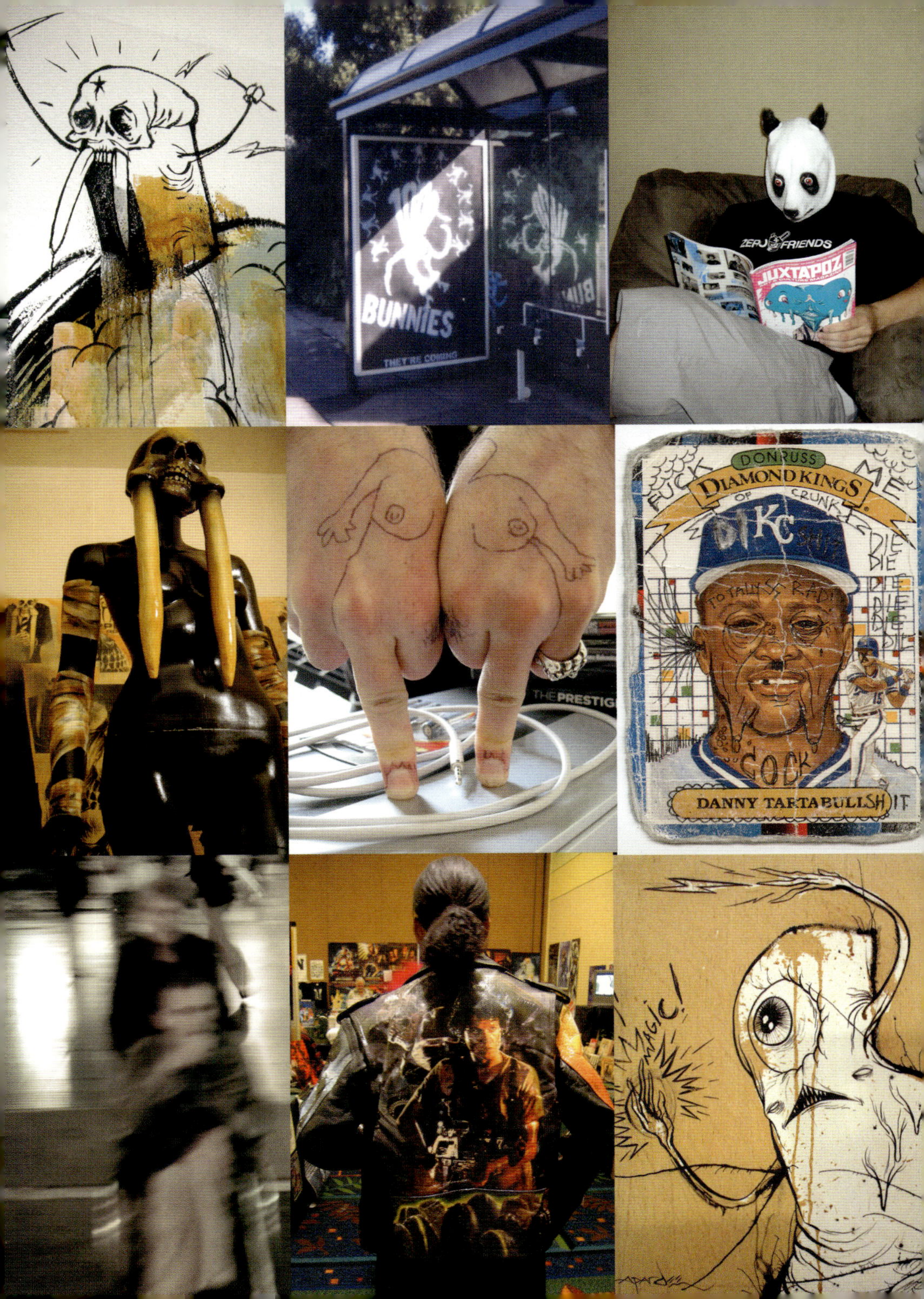

BUNNIES
THEY'RE COMING
ZERO FRIENDS
JUXTAPOZ
DONRUSS
DIAMOND KINGS
OF CRUNK
FUCK ME
DIE DIE DIE DIE DIE
TOTALLY RAD
COCK
DANNY TARTABULLSHIT
MAGIC!

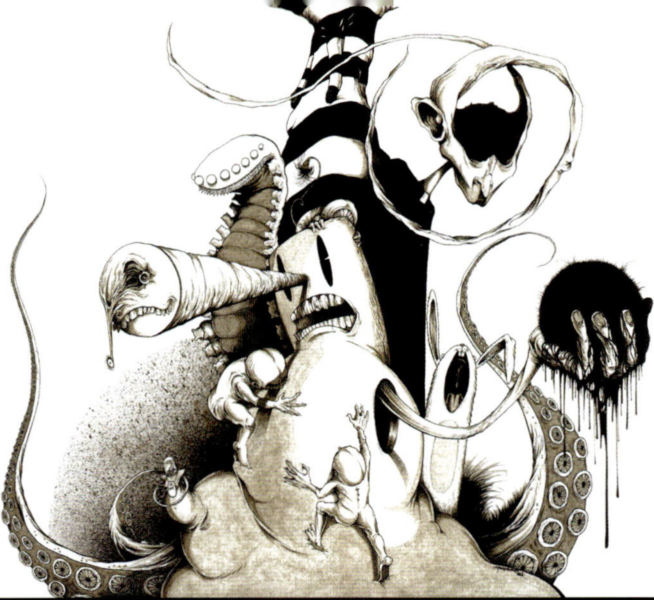

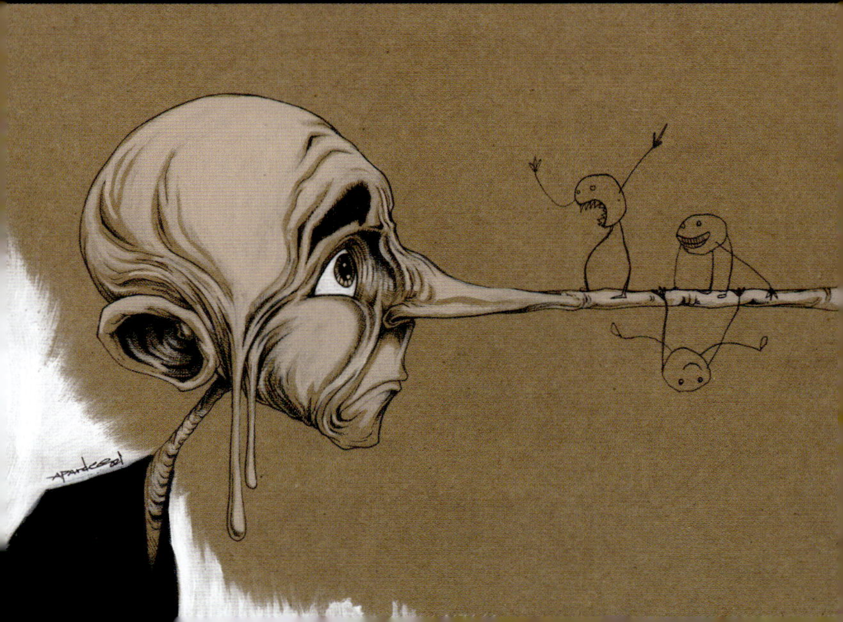

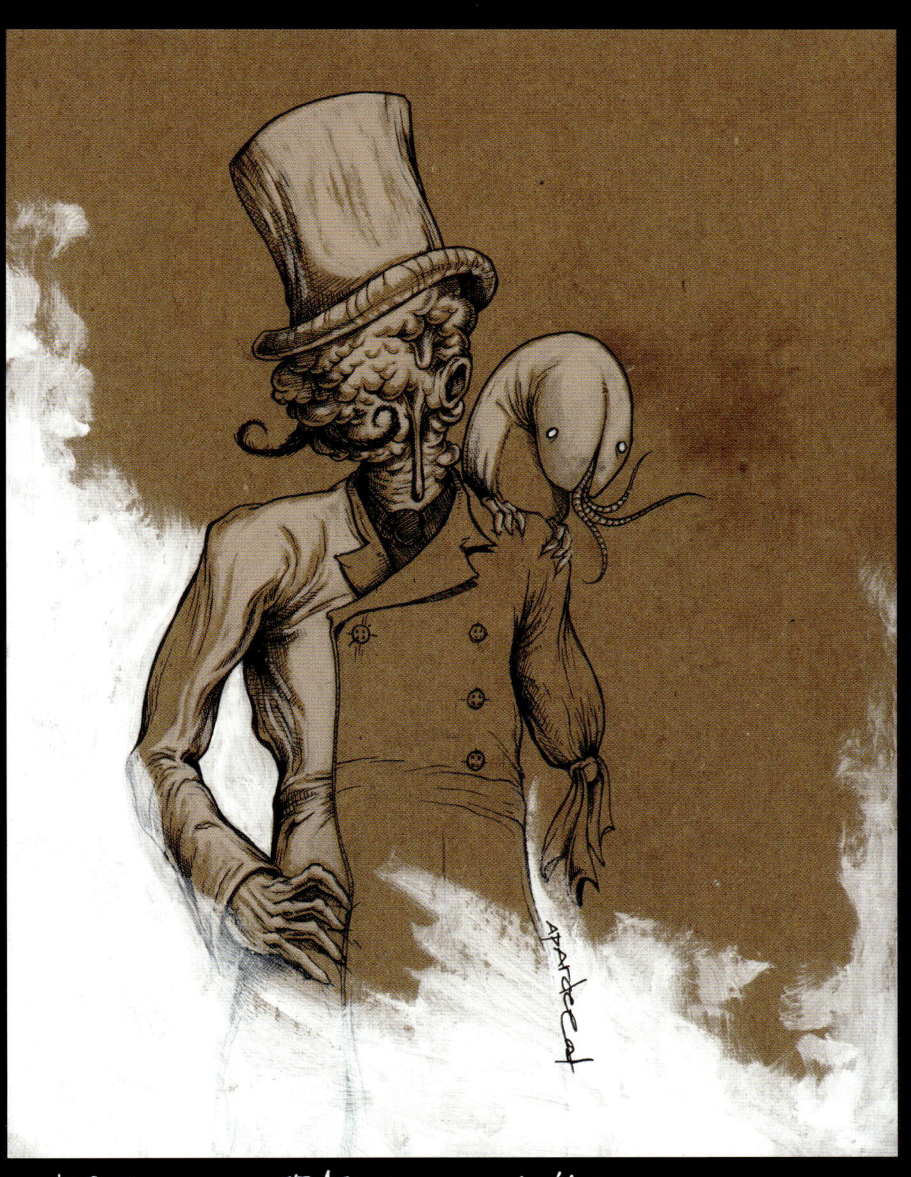

FOR 17 YEARS, I WAS
OBSESSED WITH THE PLAGUE.

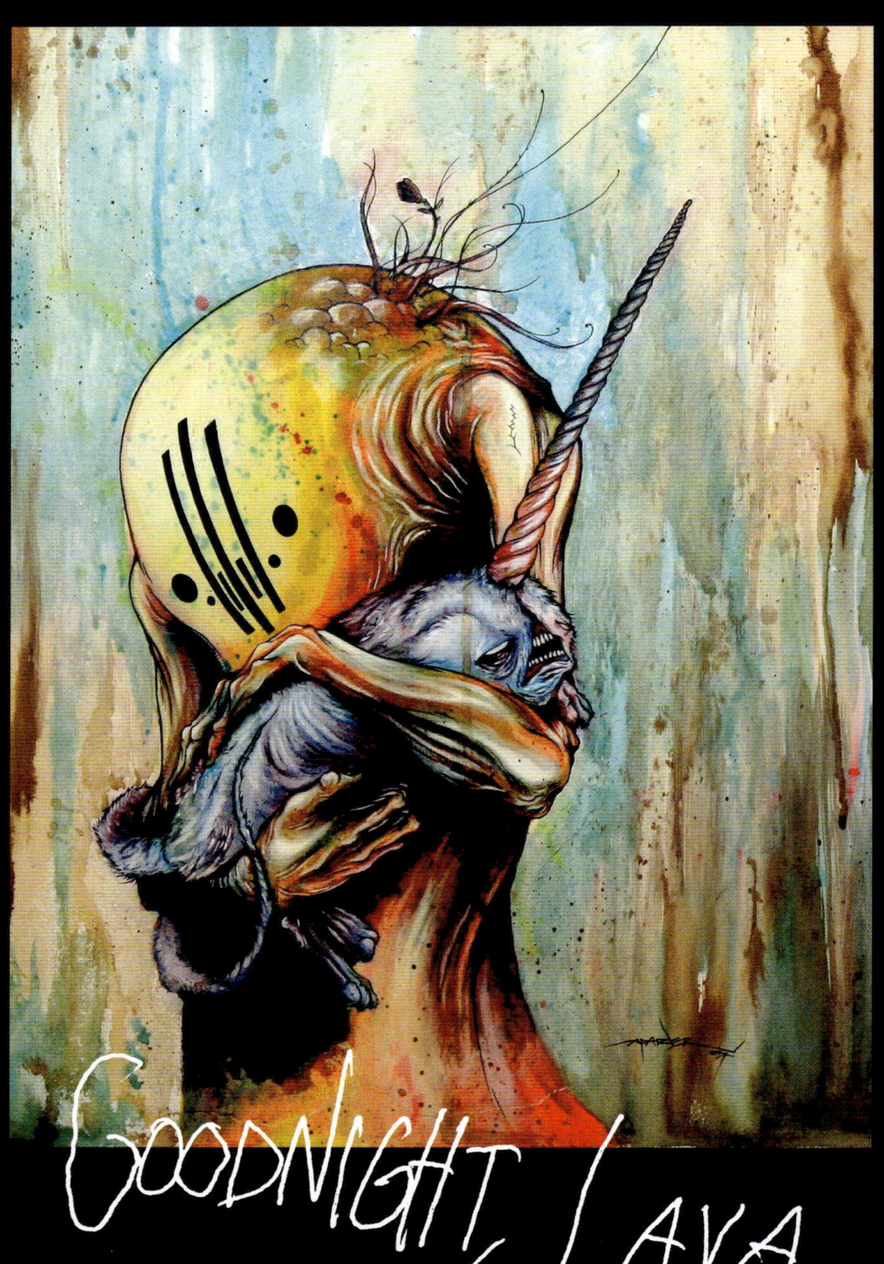

GOODNIGHT, LAVA.

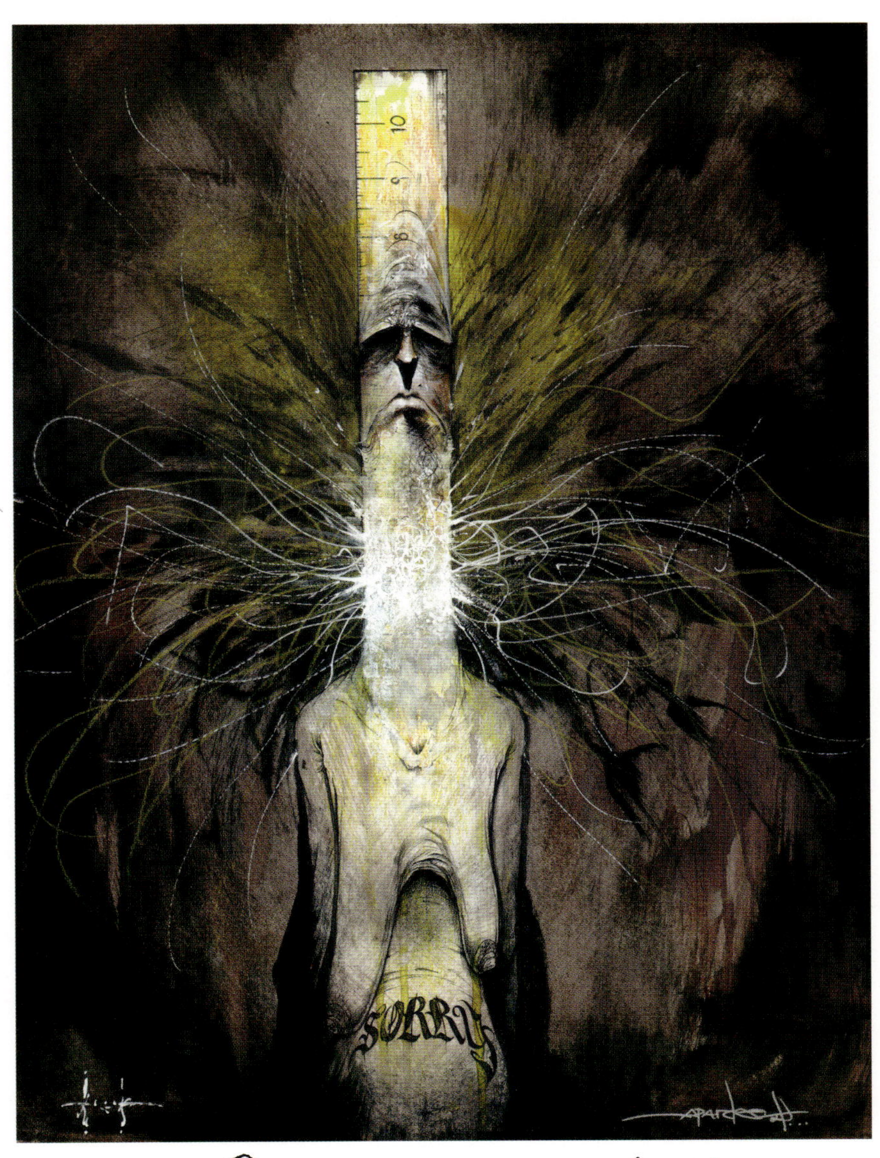

COLLABORATION WITH SAM KIETH.

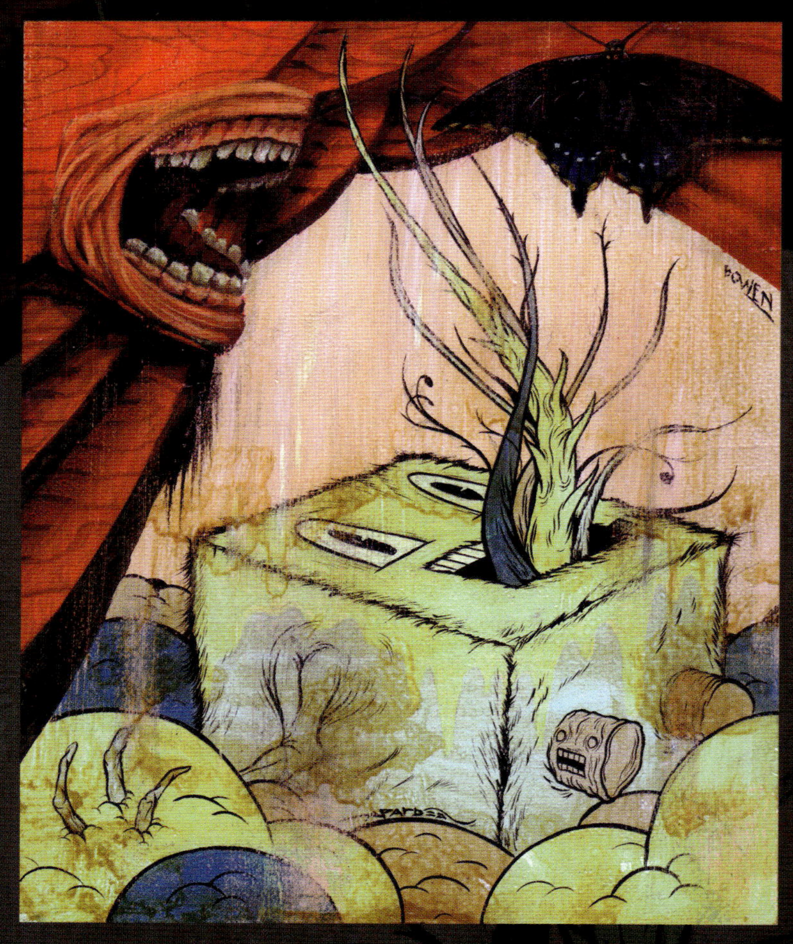

COLLABORATION WITH ROBERT BOWEN

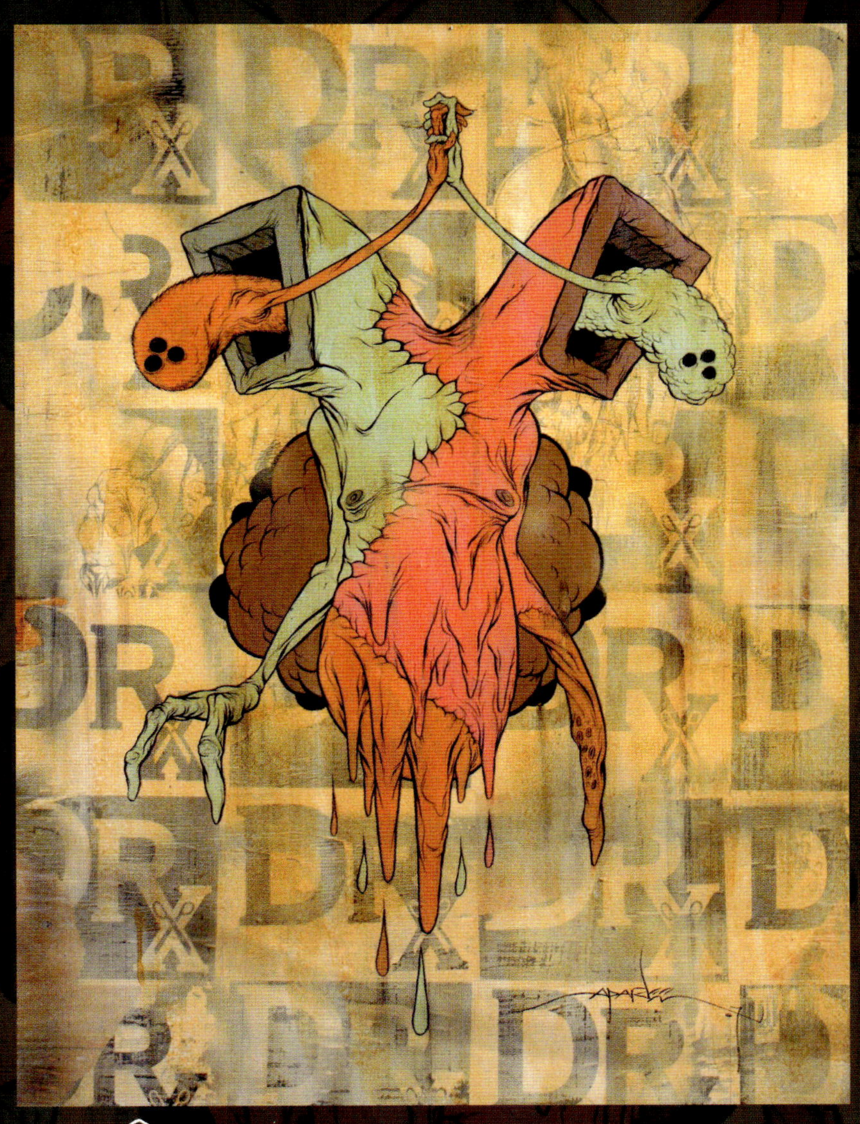

COLLABORATION WITH DR. X.

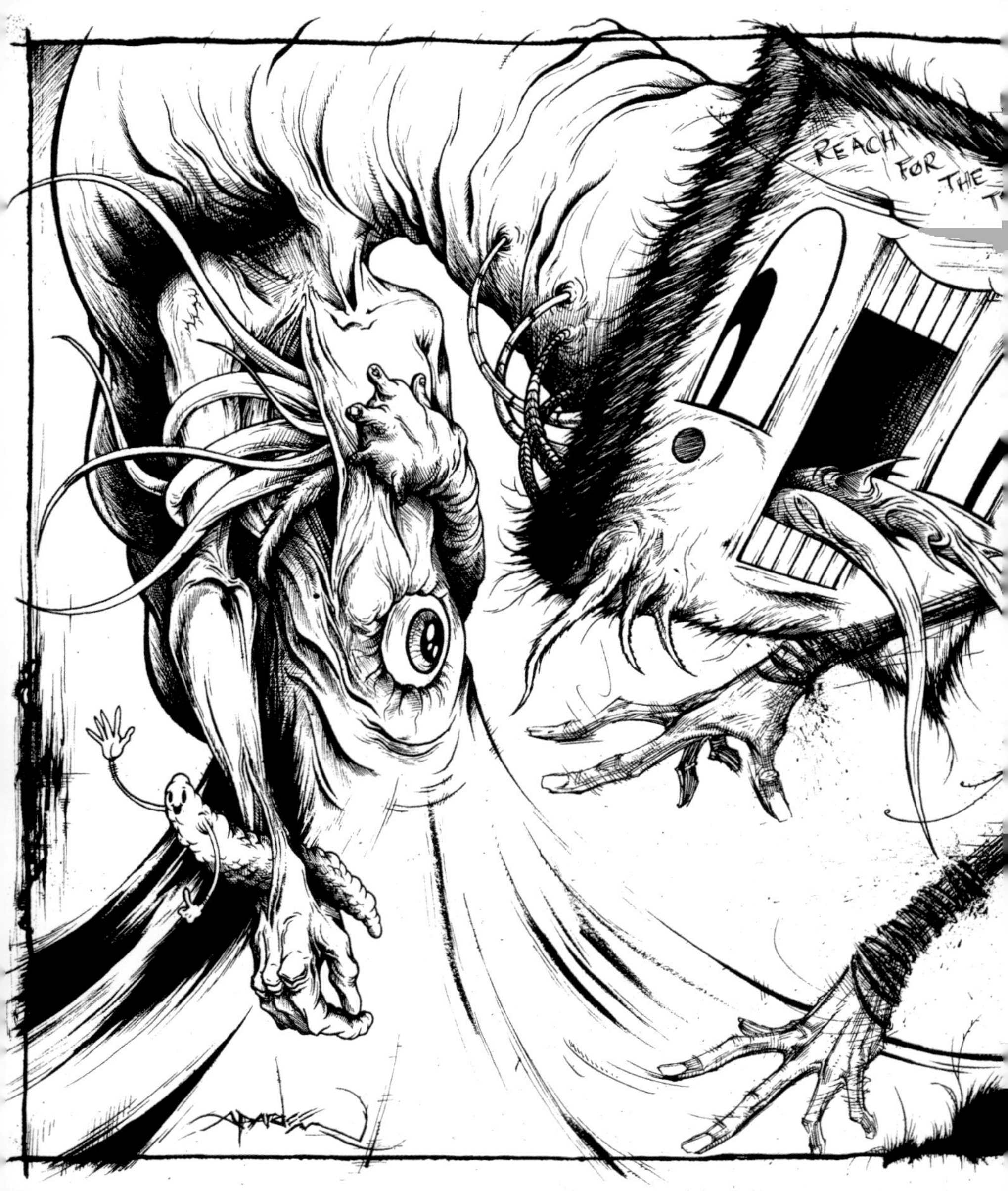
REACH FOR THE

COLLABORATION WITH JON WAYSHAK

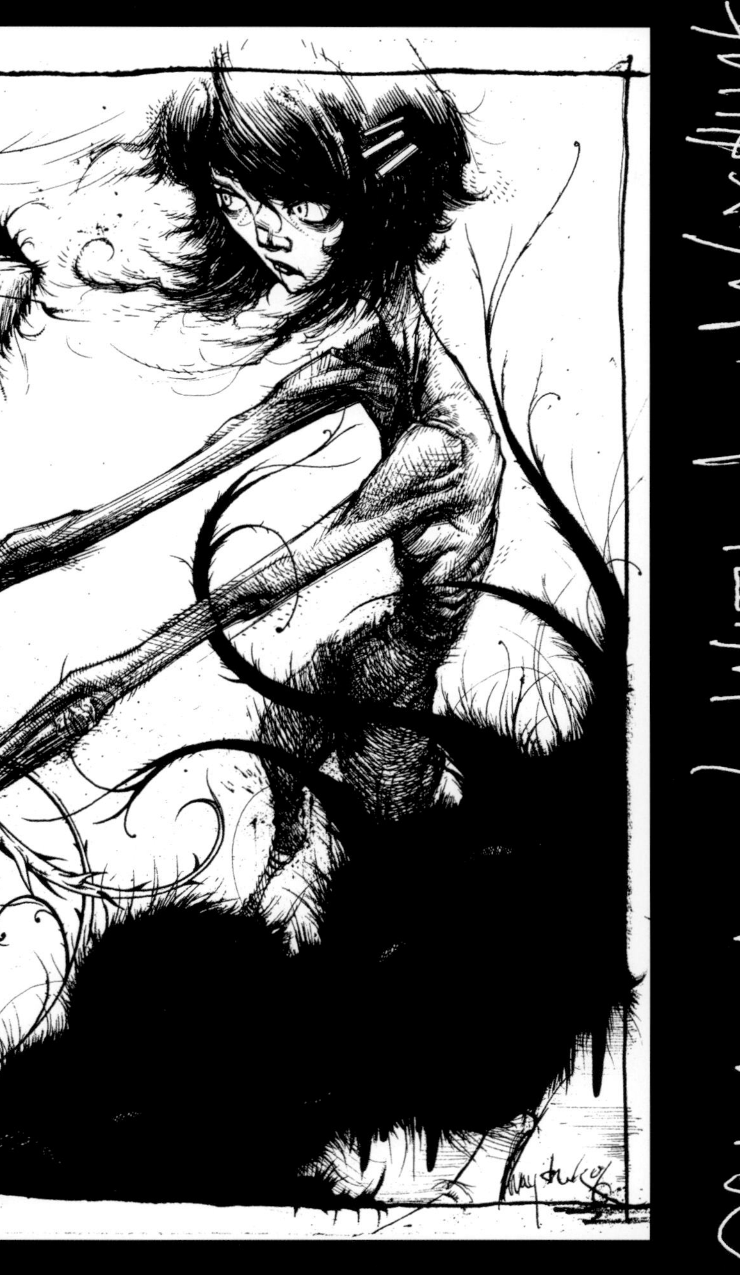

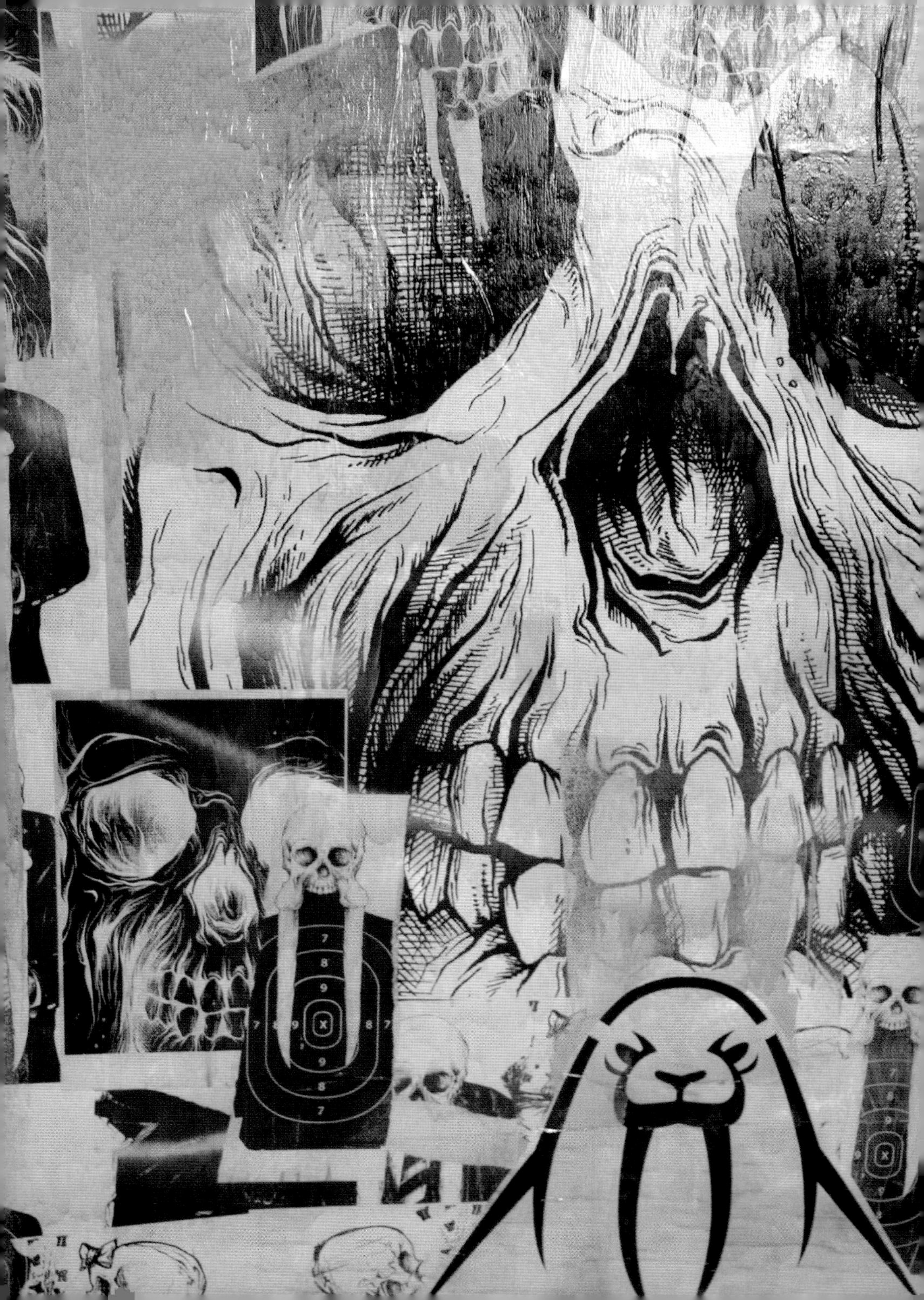

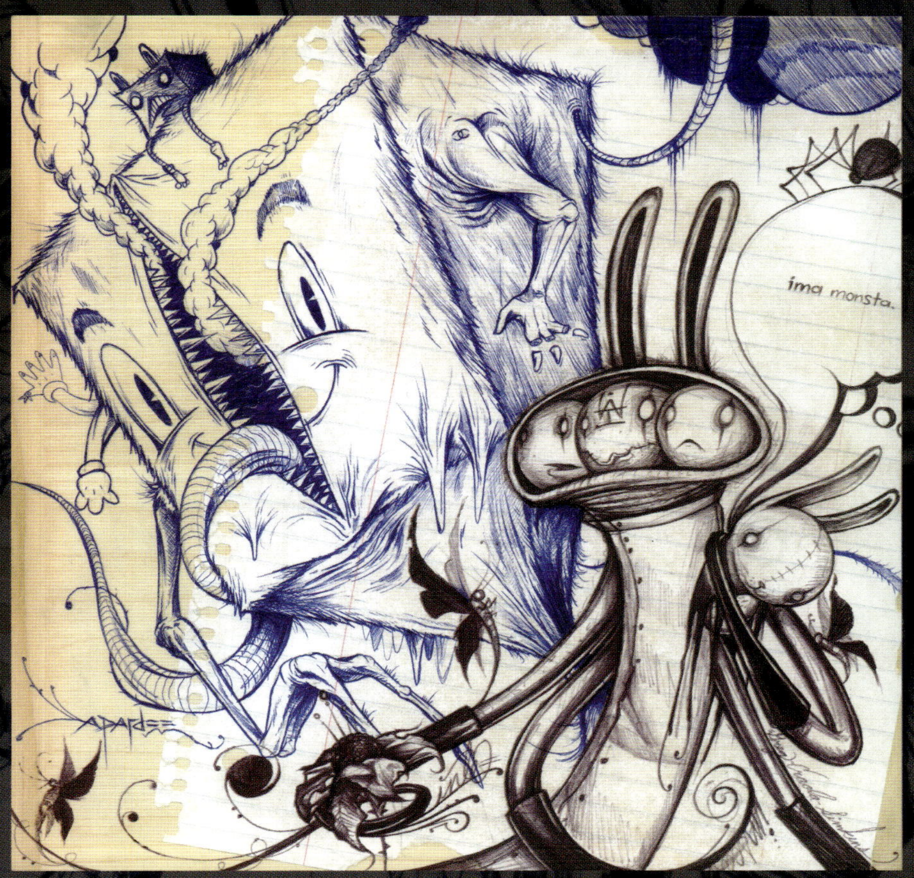

COLLABORATION WITH GREG "CRAOLA" SIMKINS

next page, too.

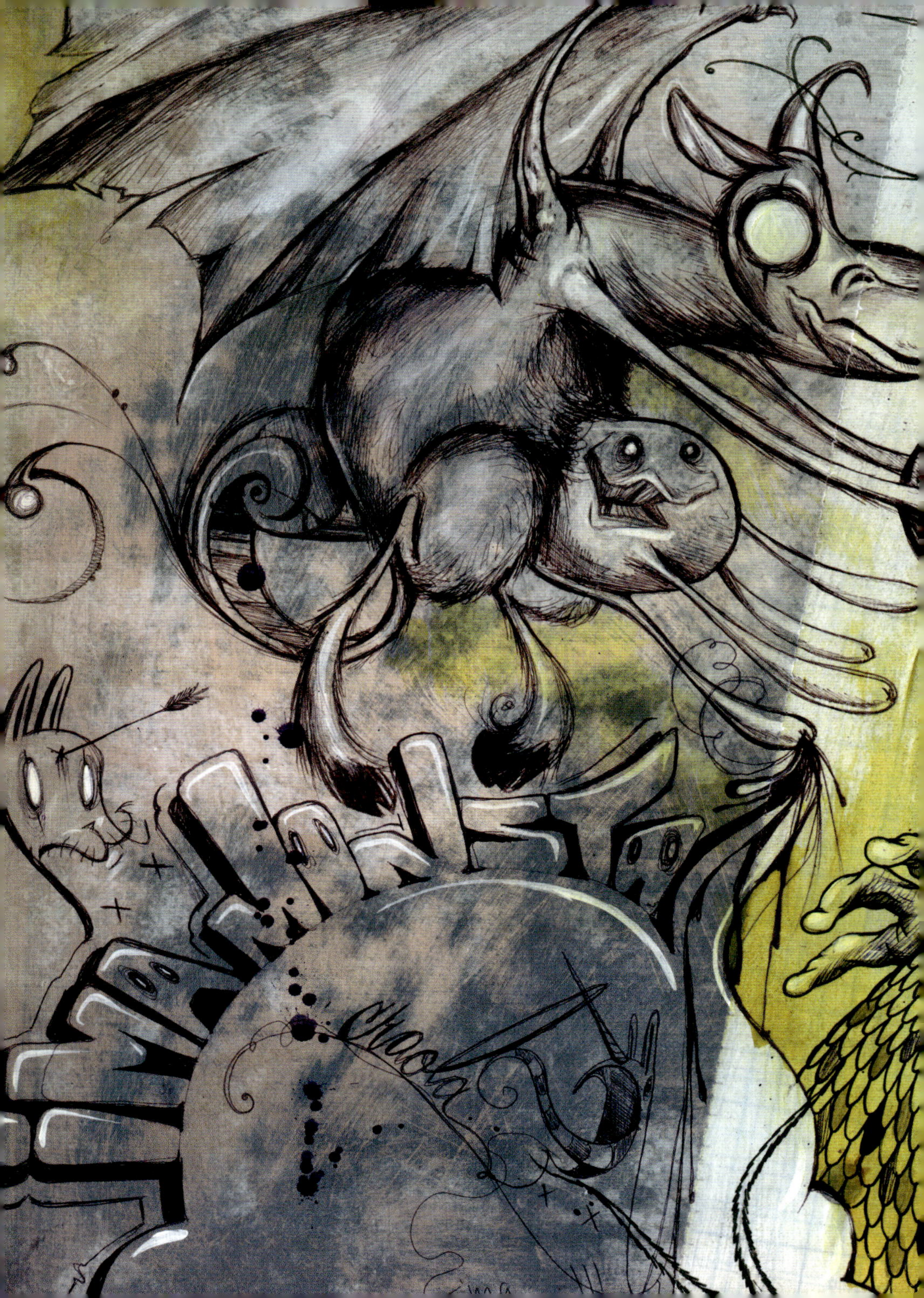

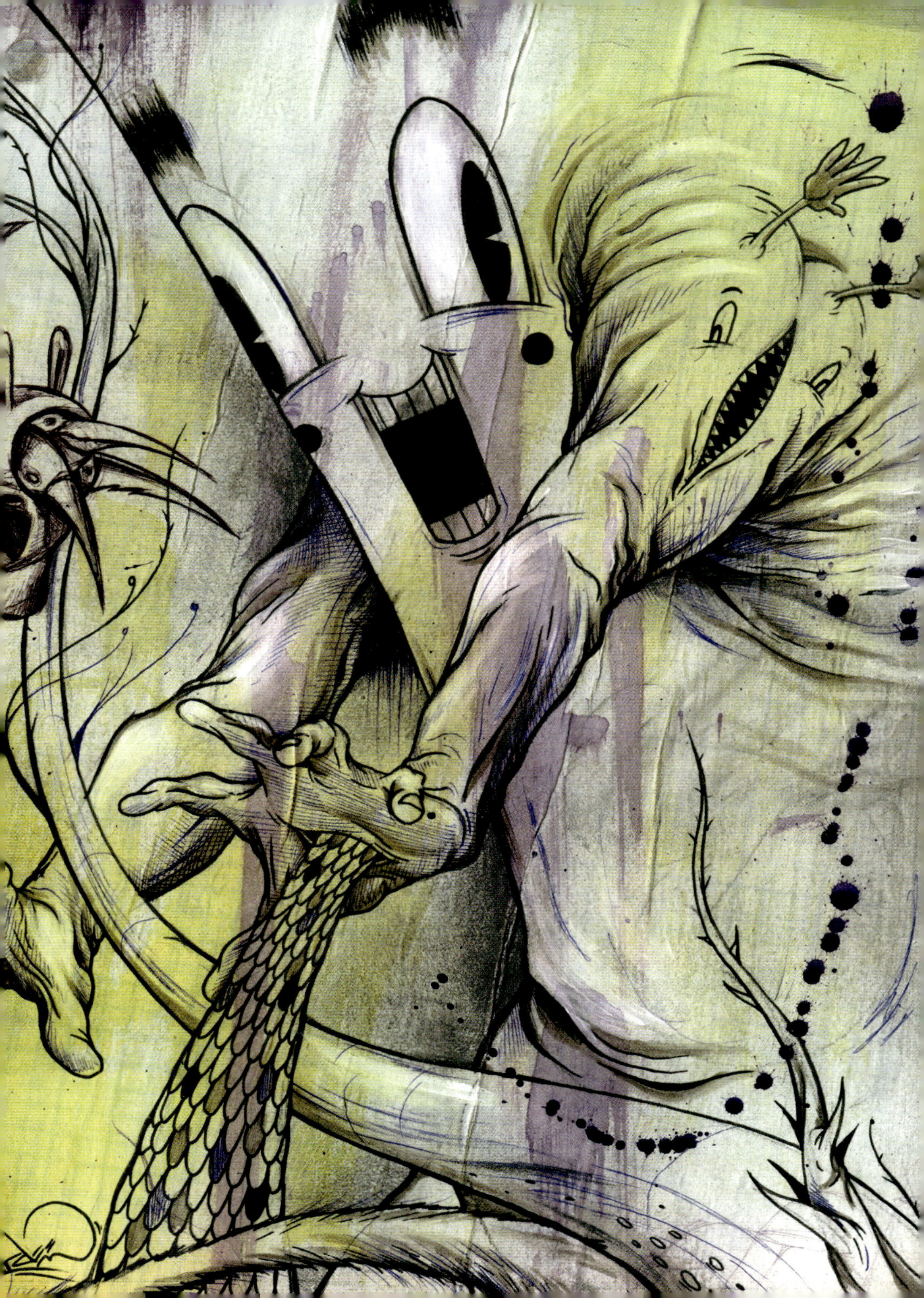

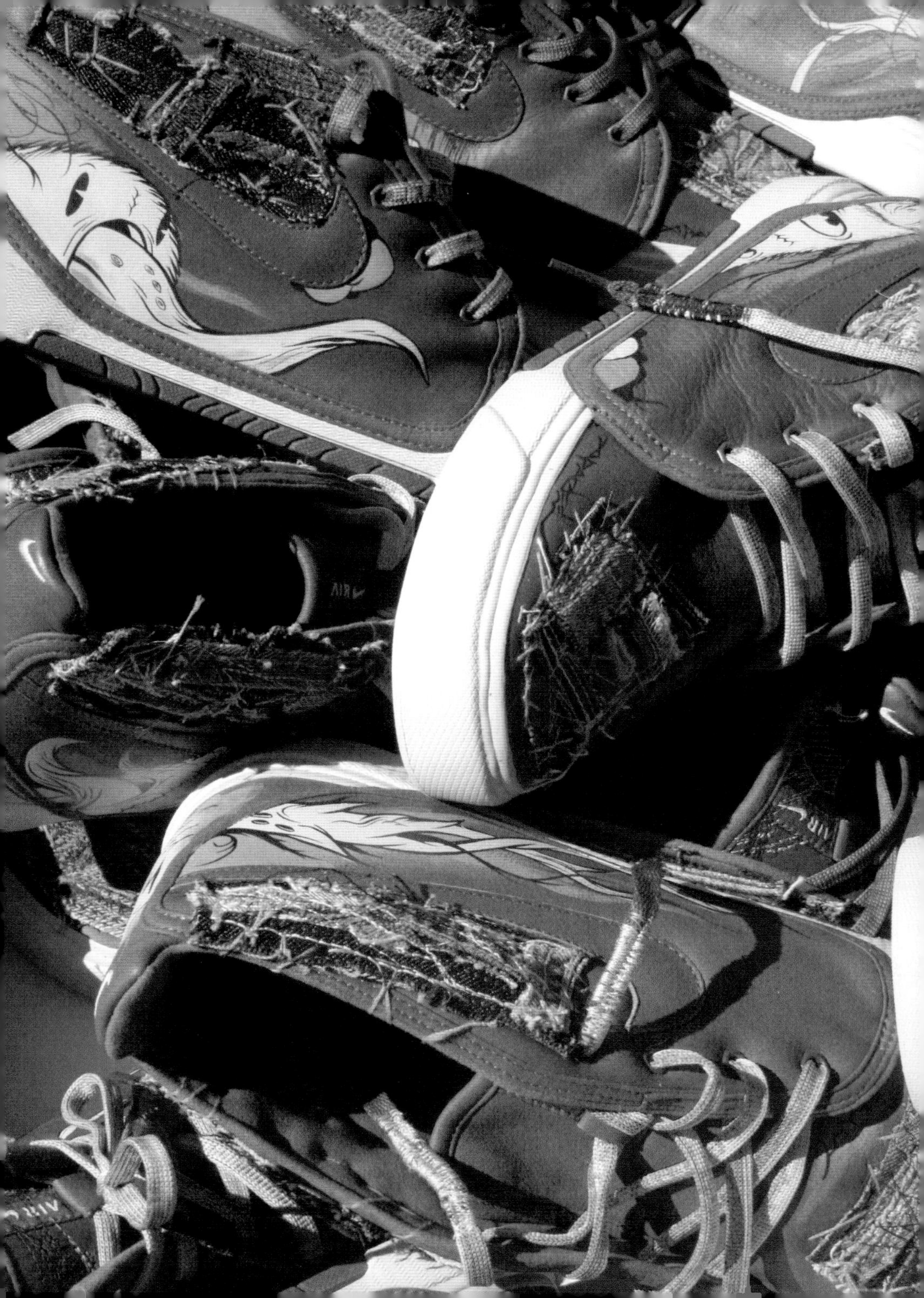

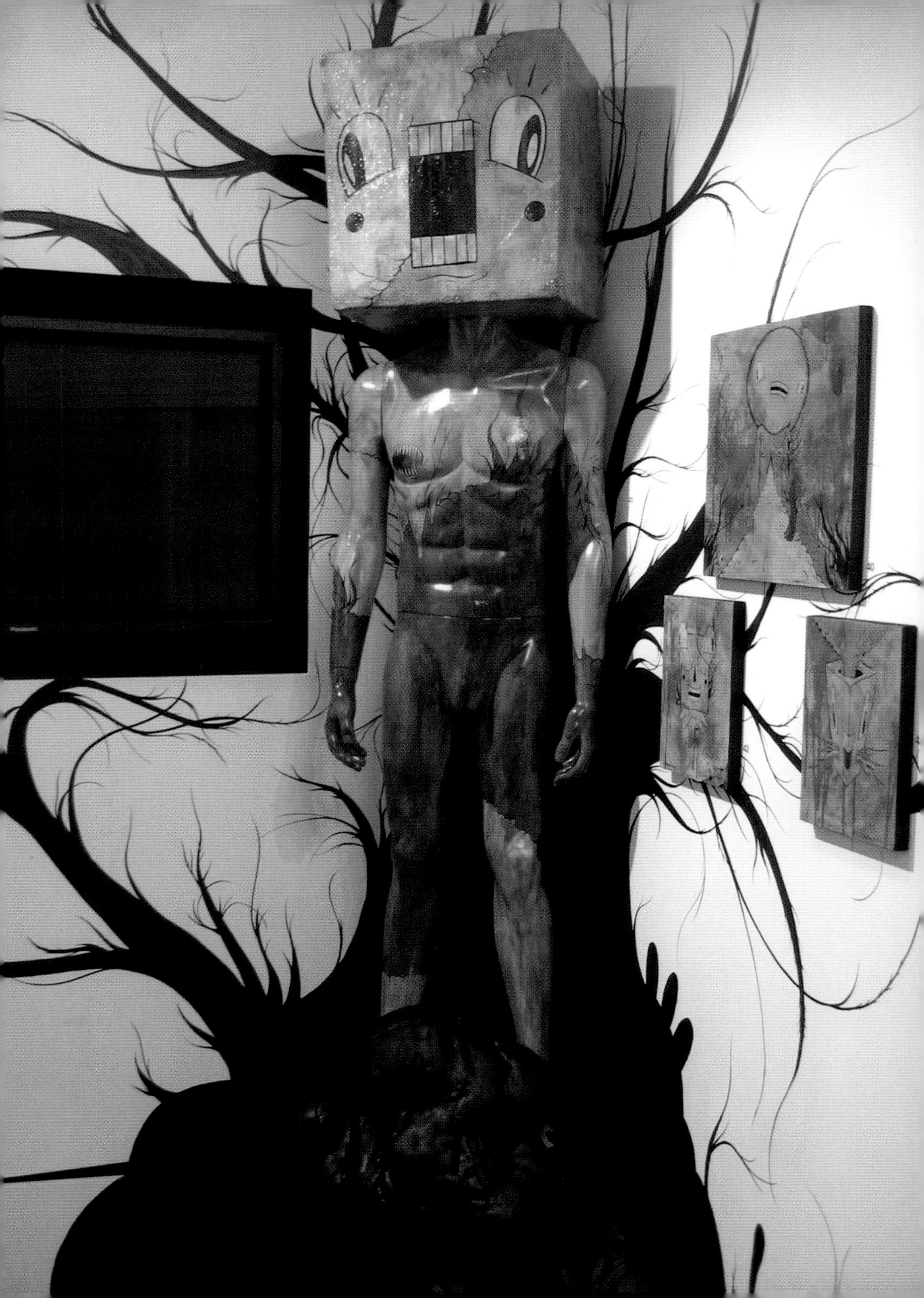

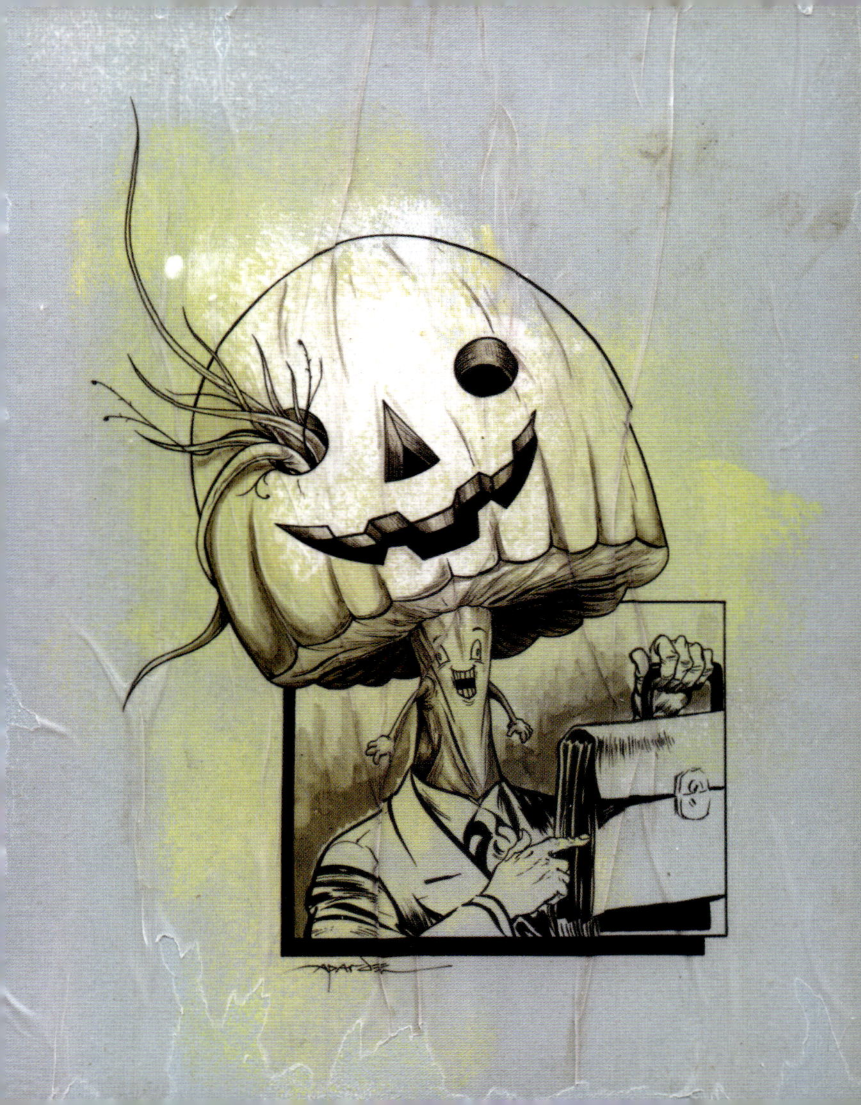

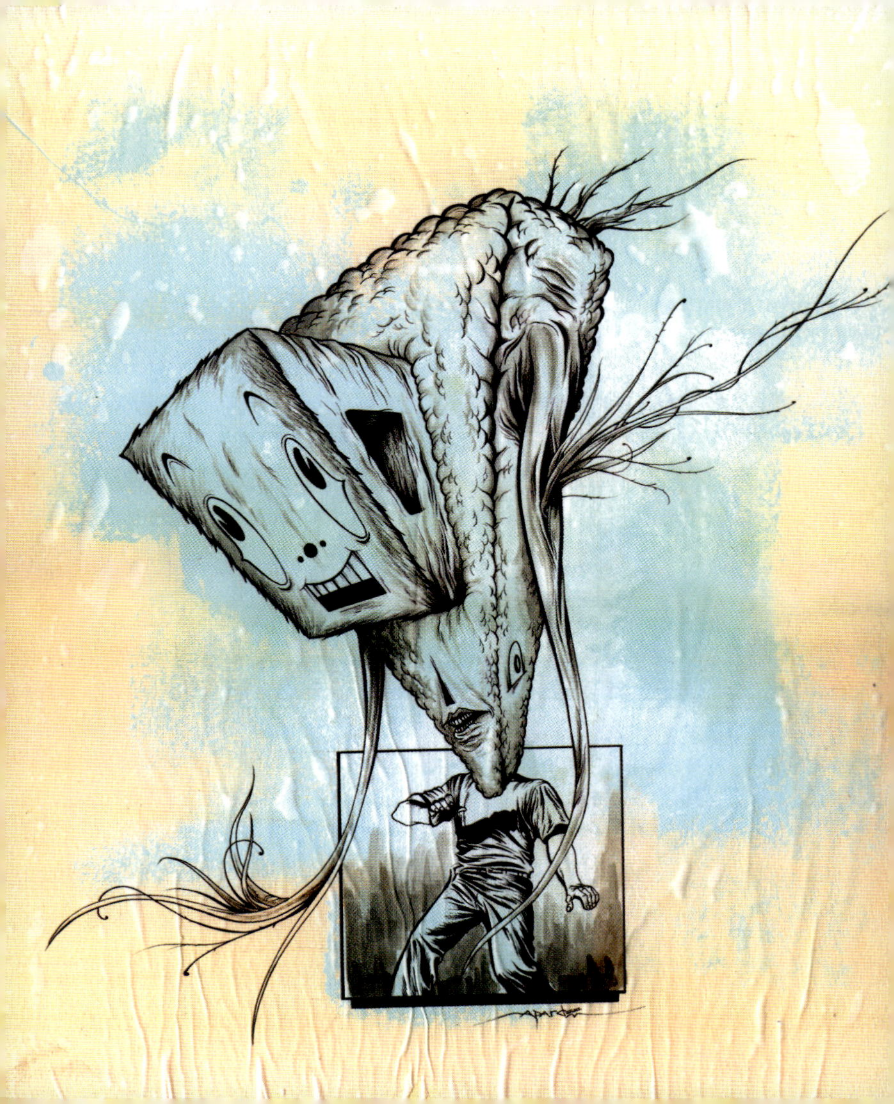

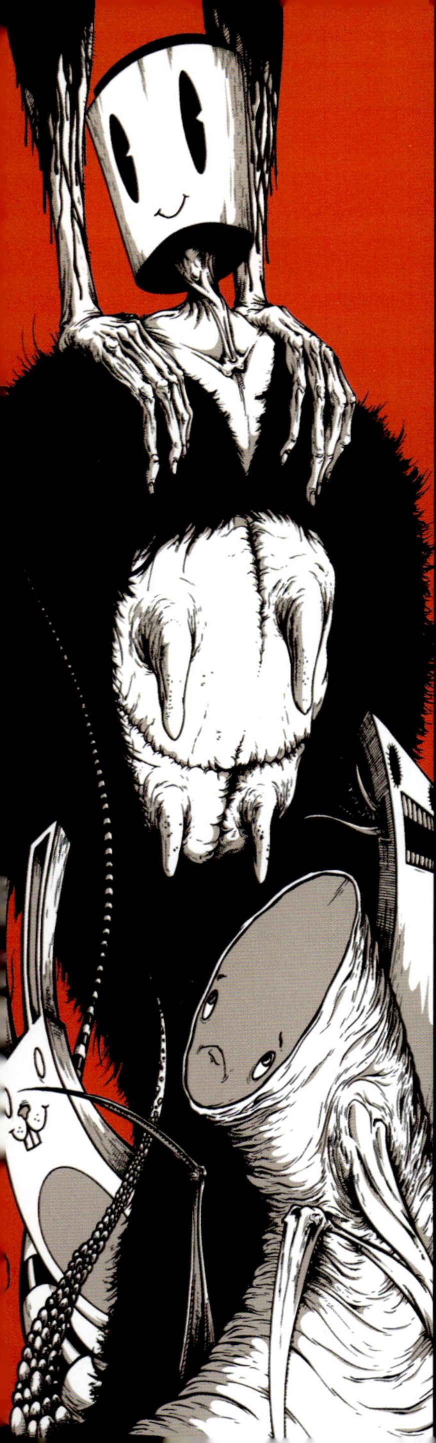

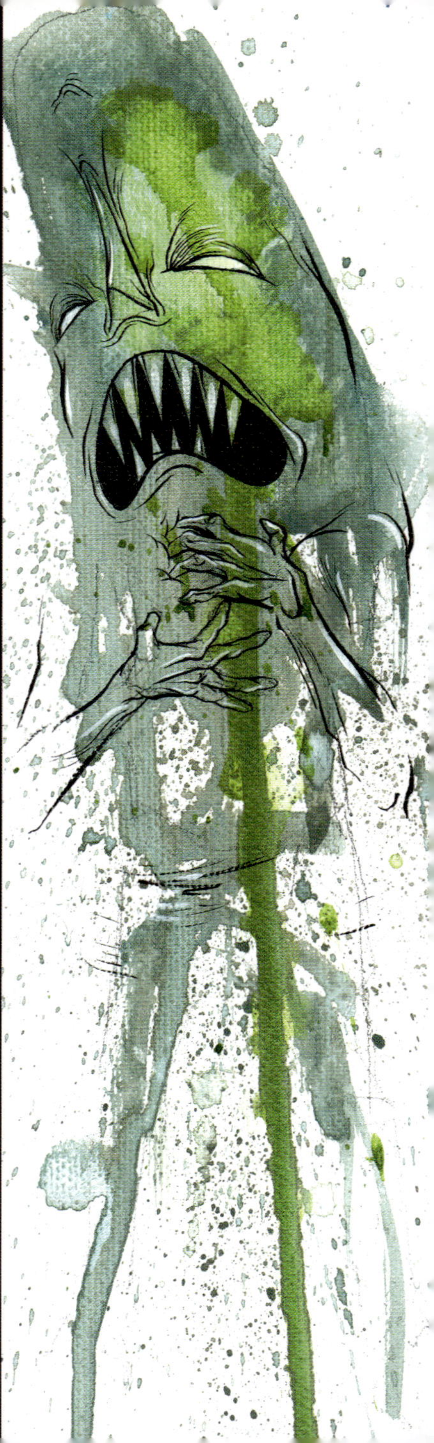

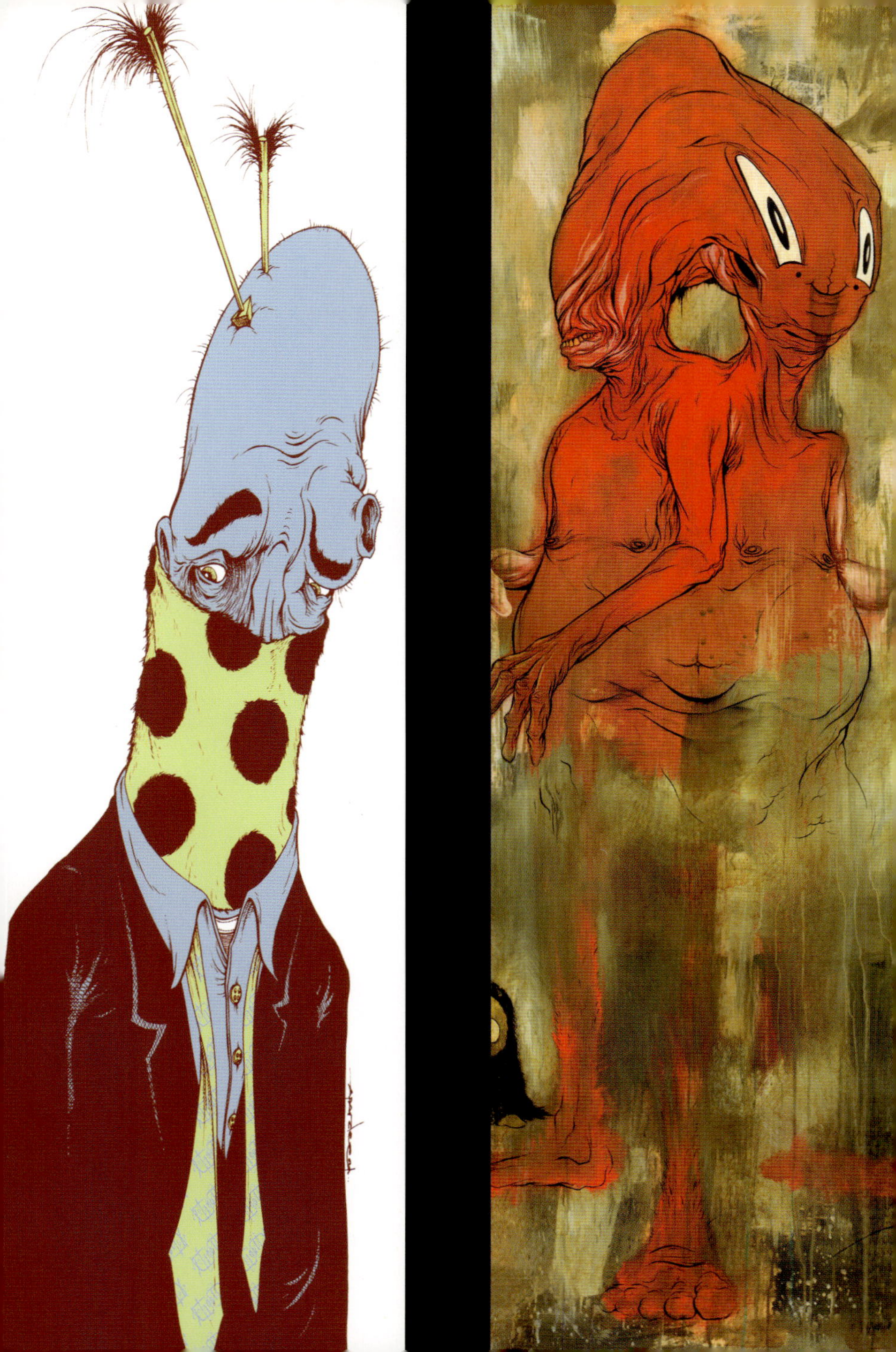

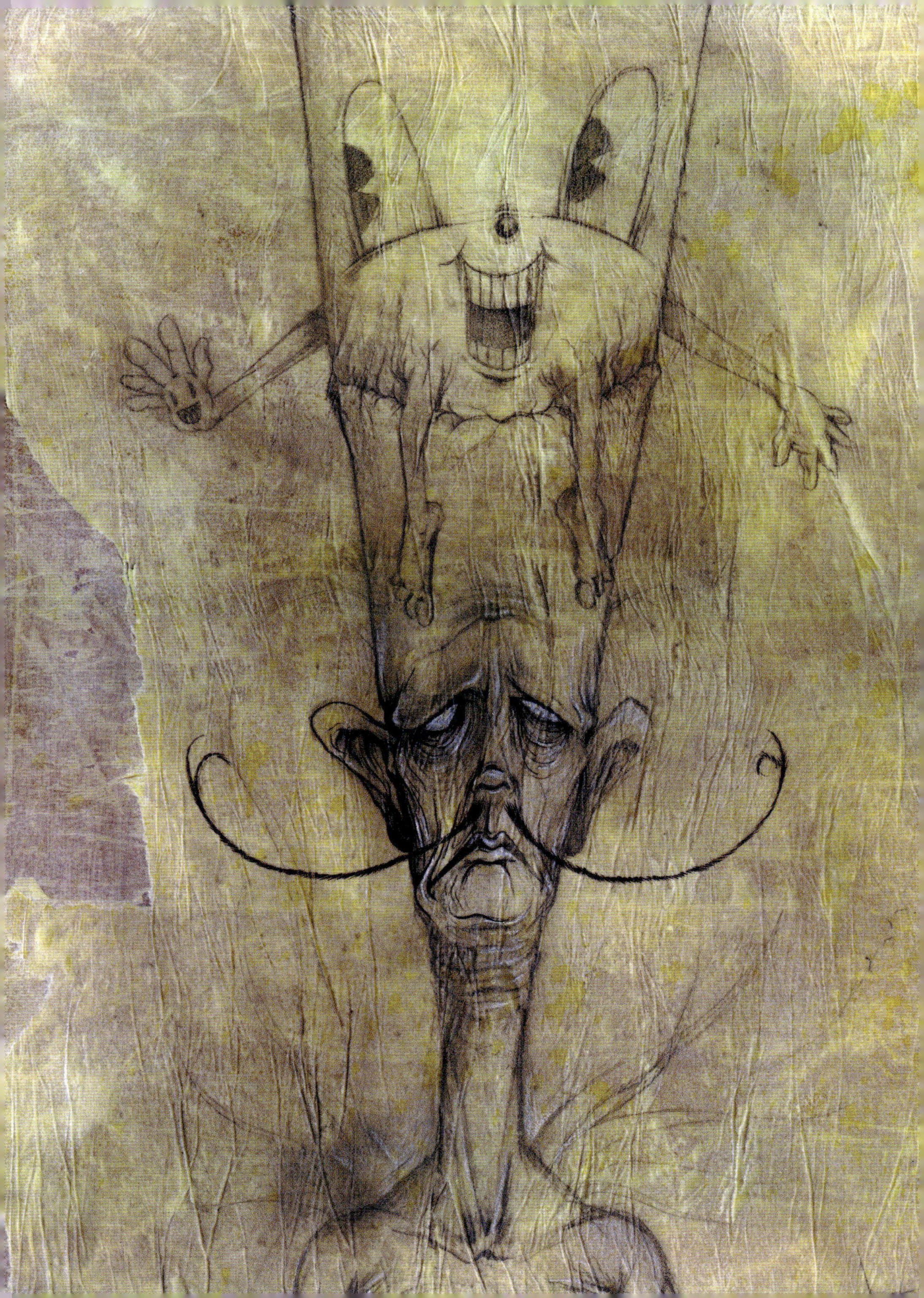

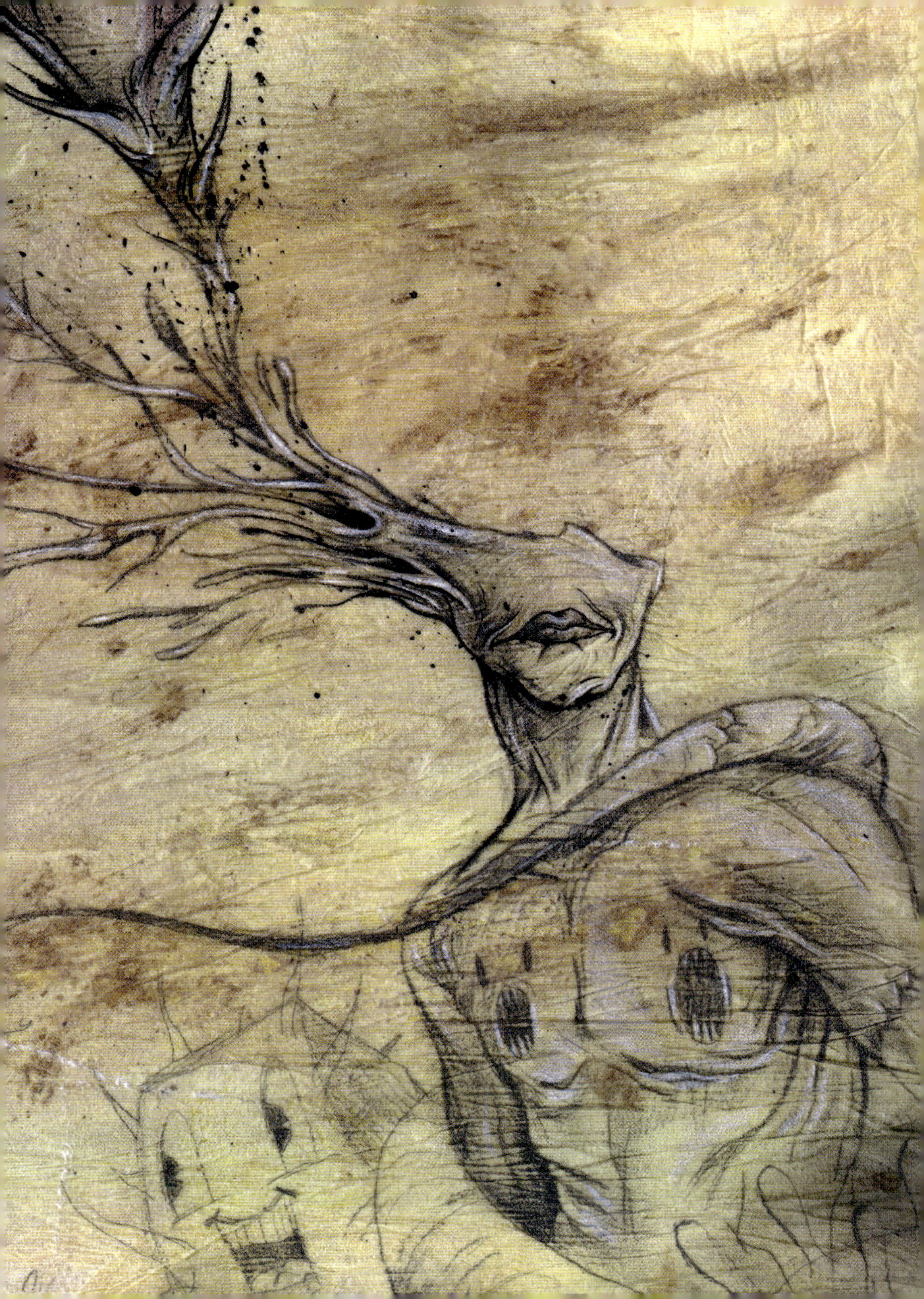

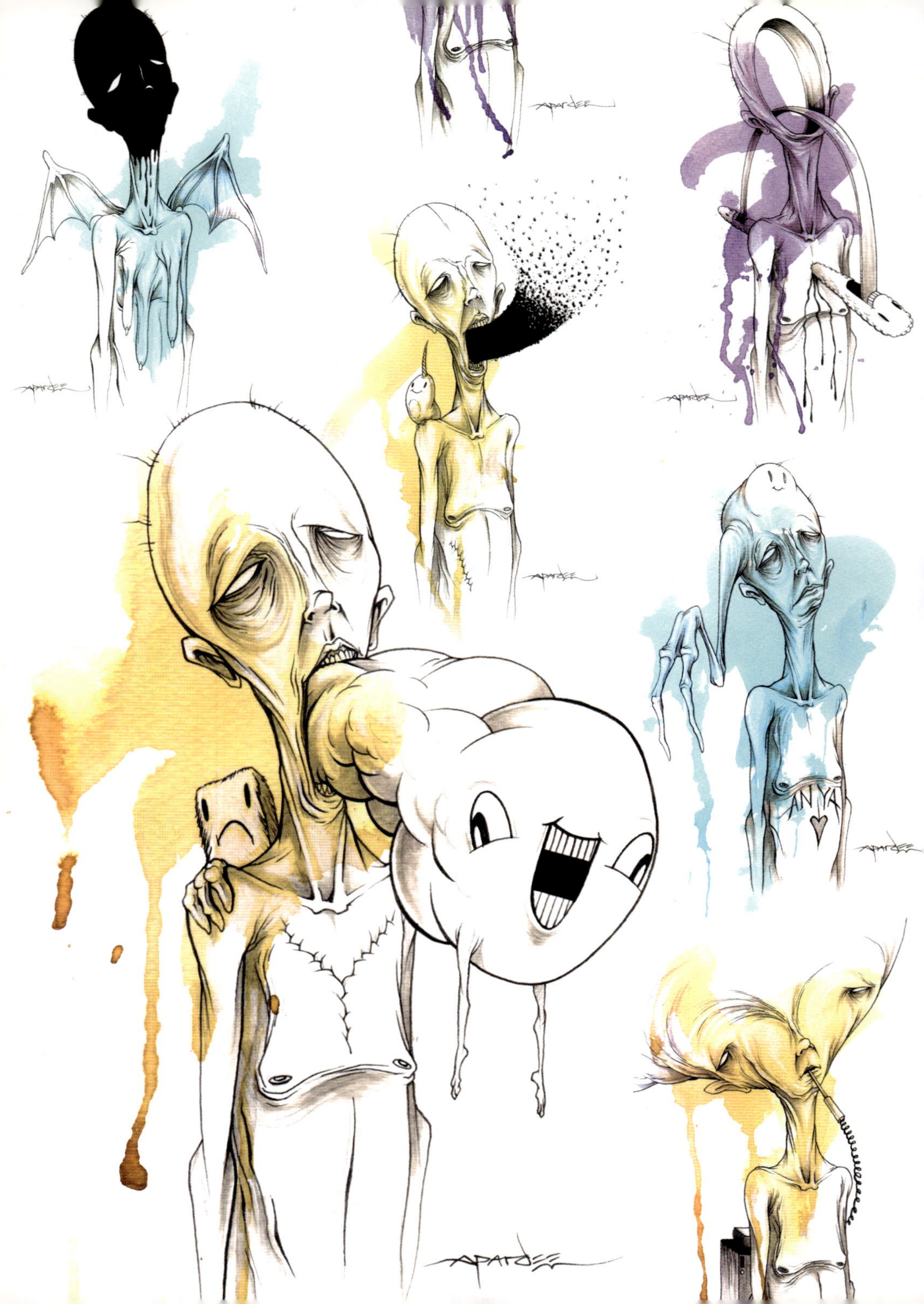
AN YA

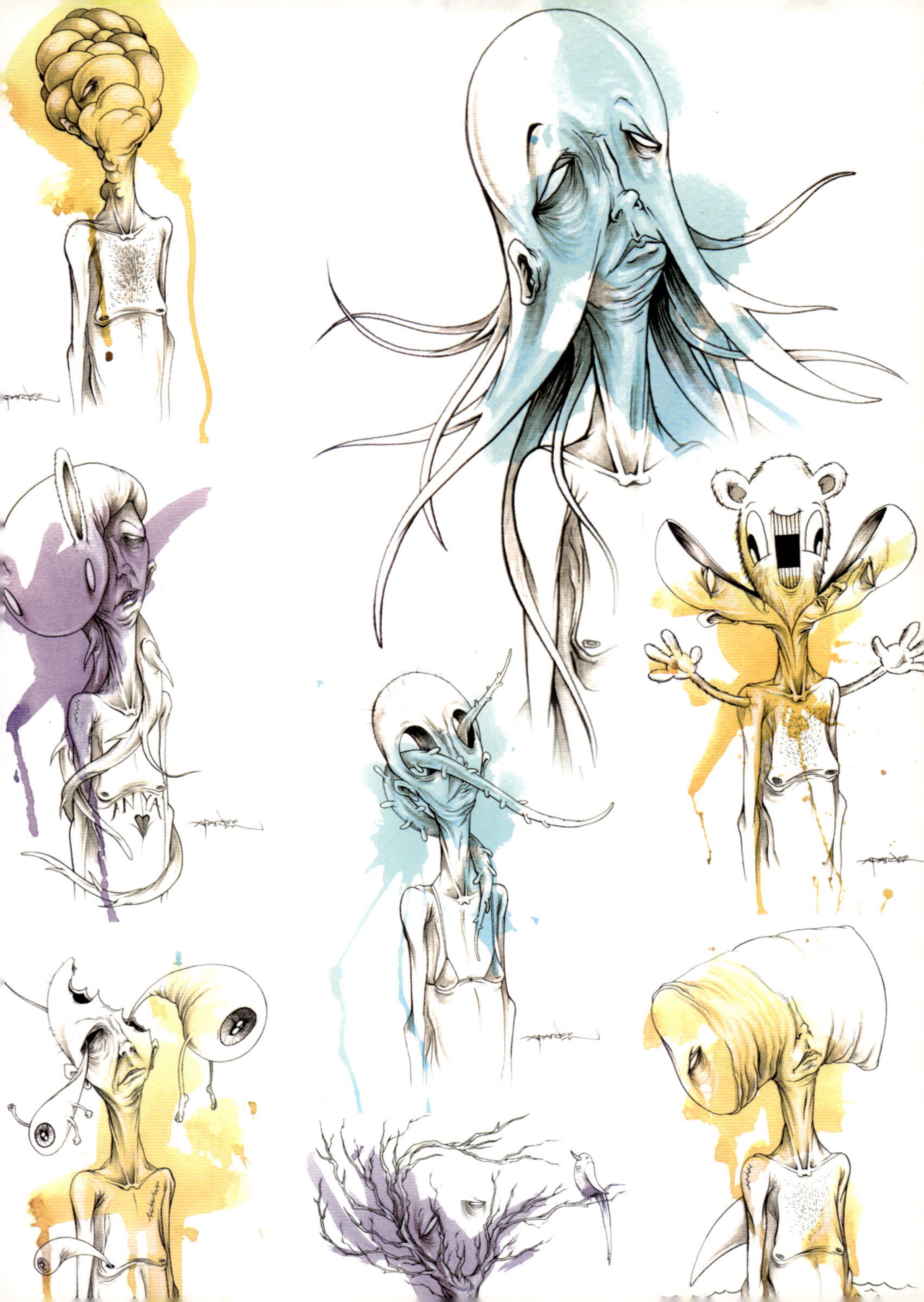
ANYA

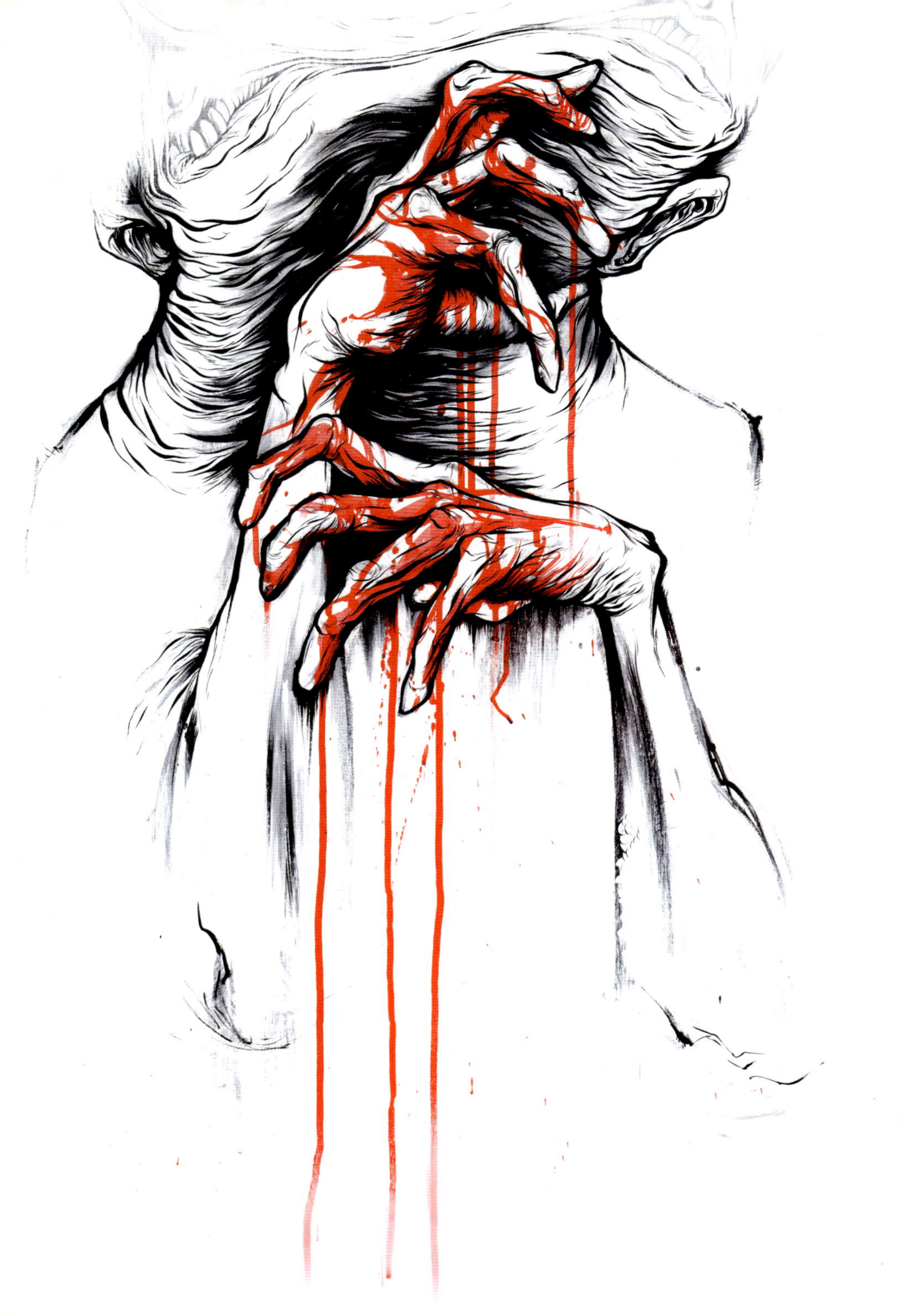

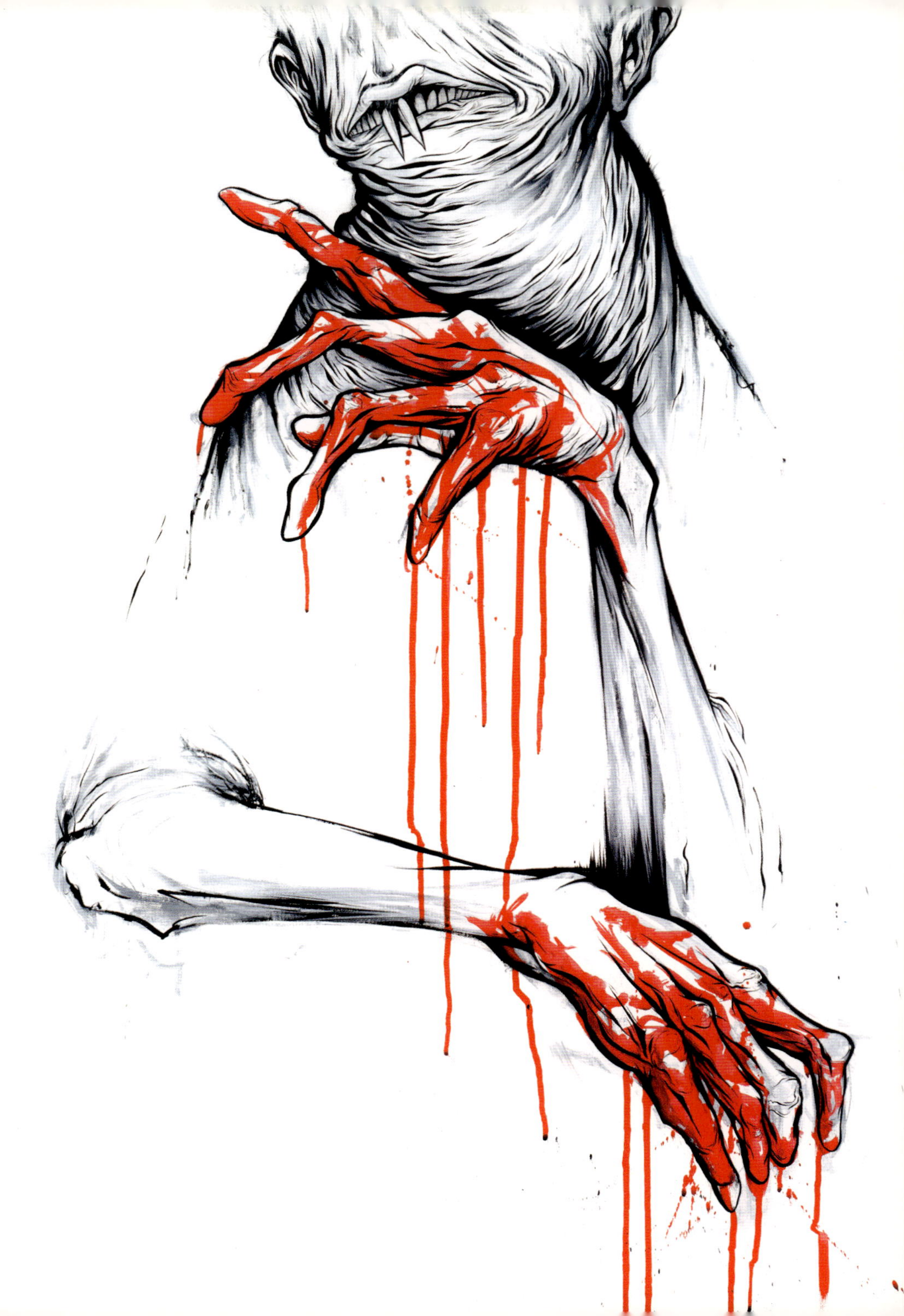

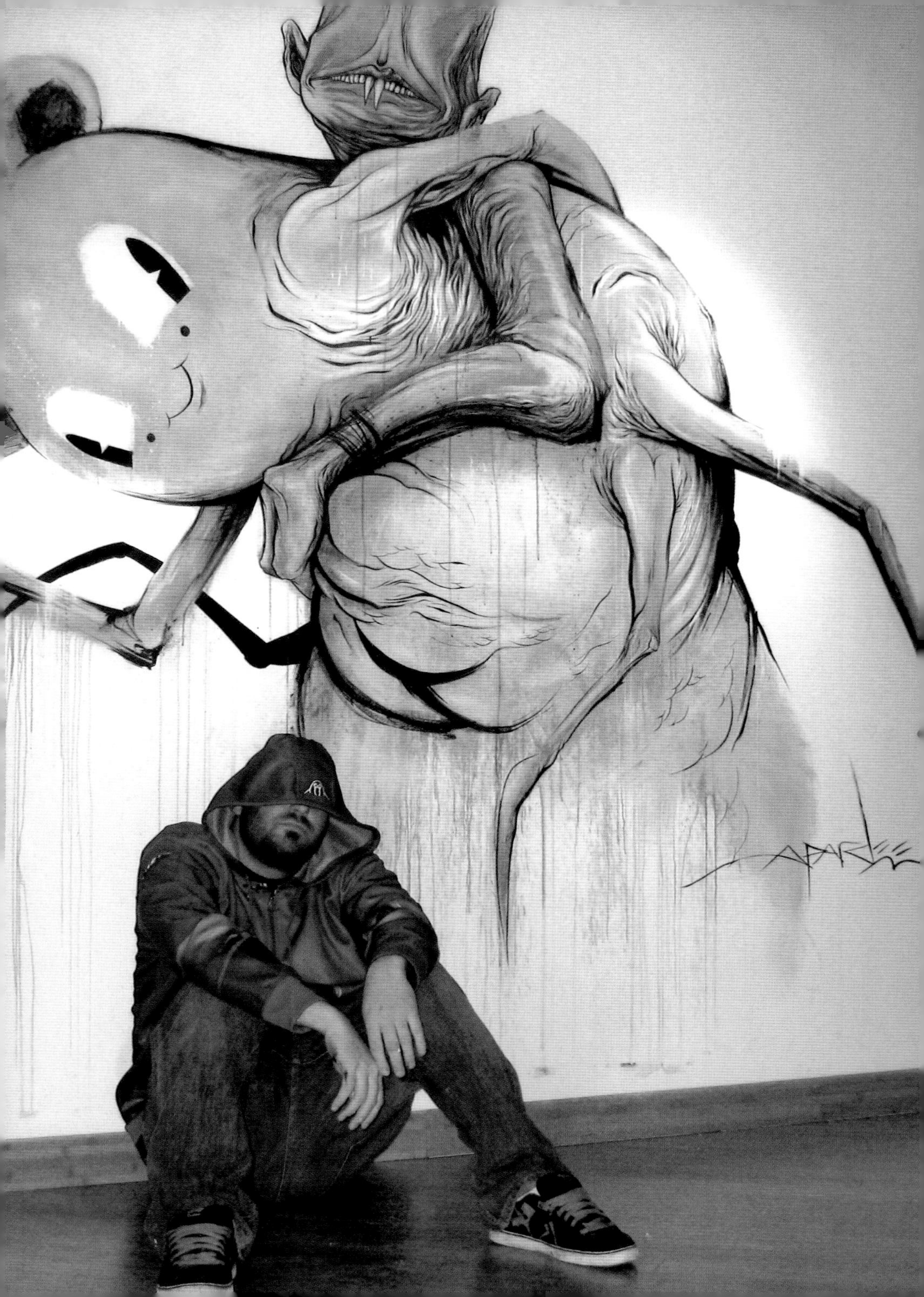

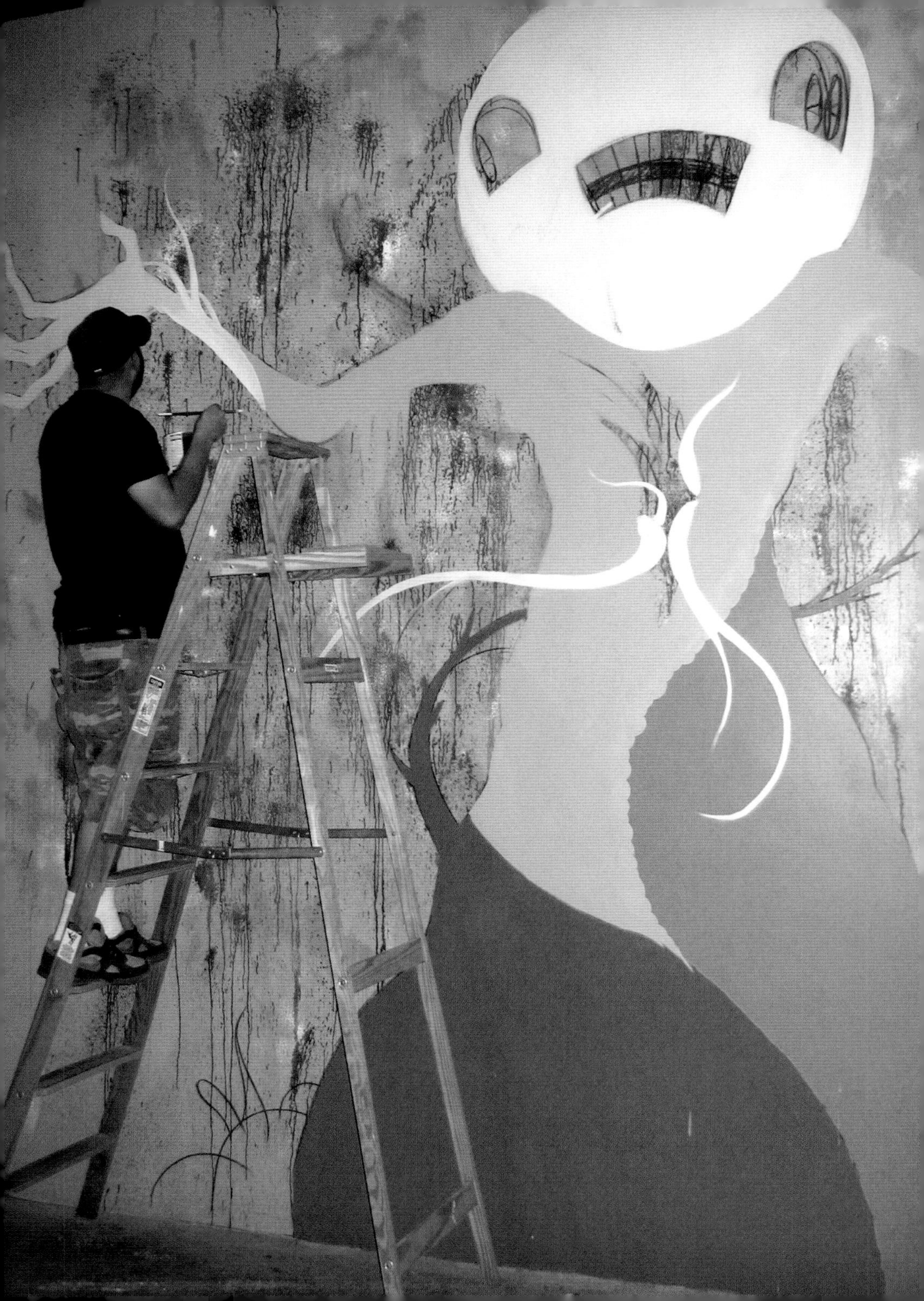

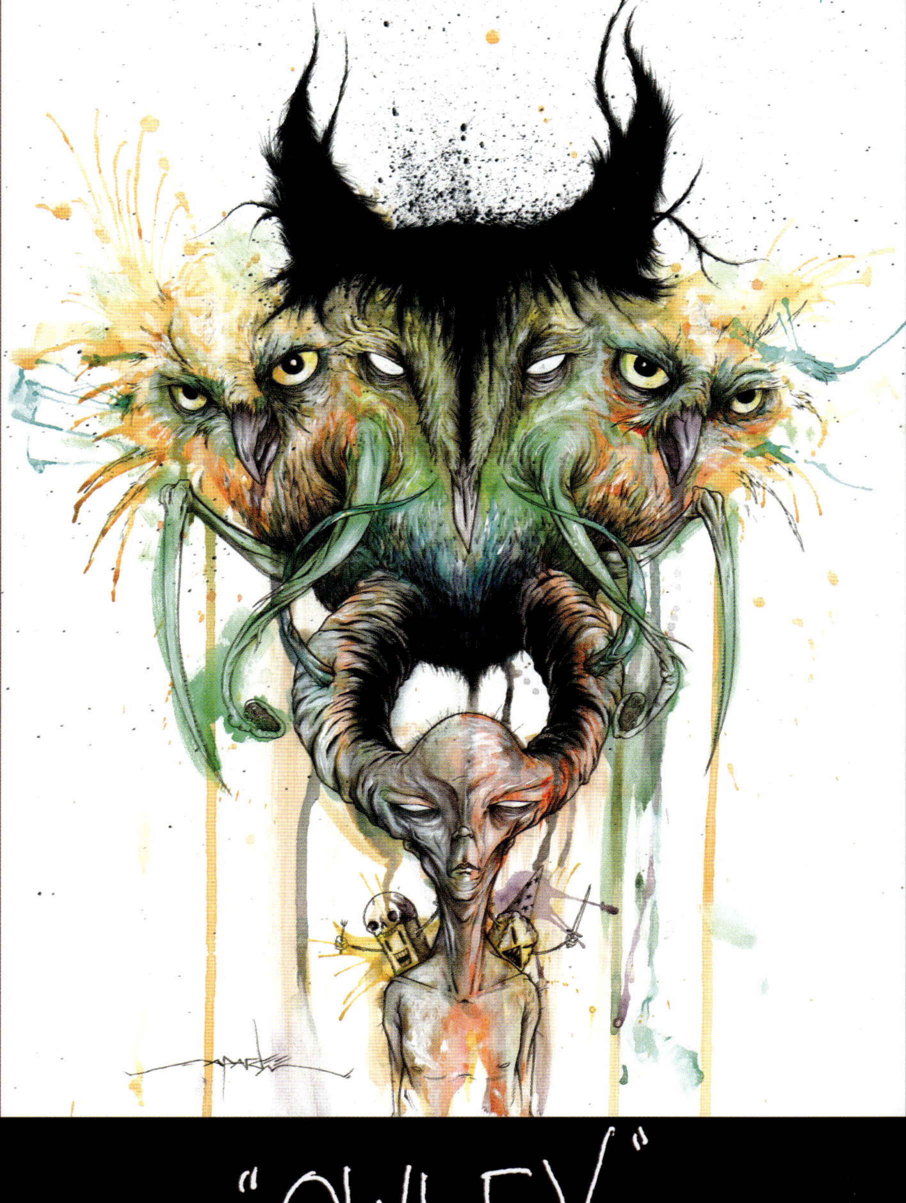

"OWLEX"

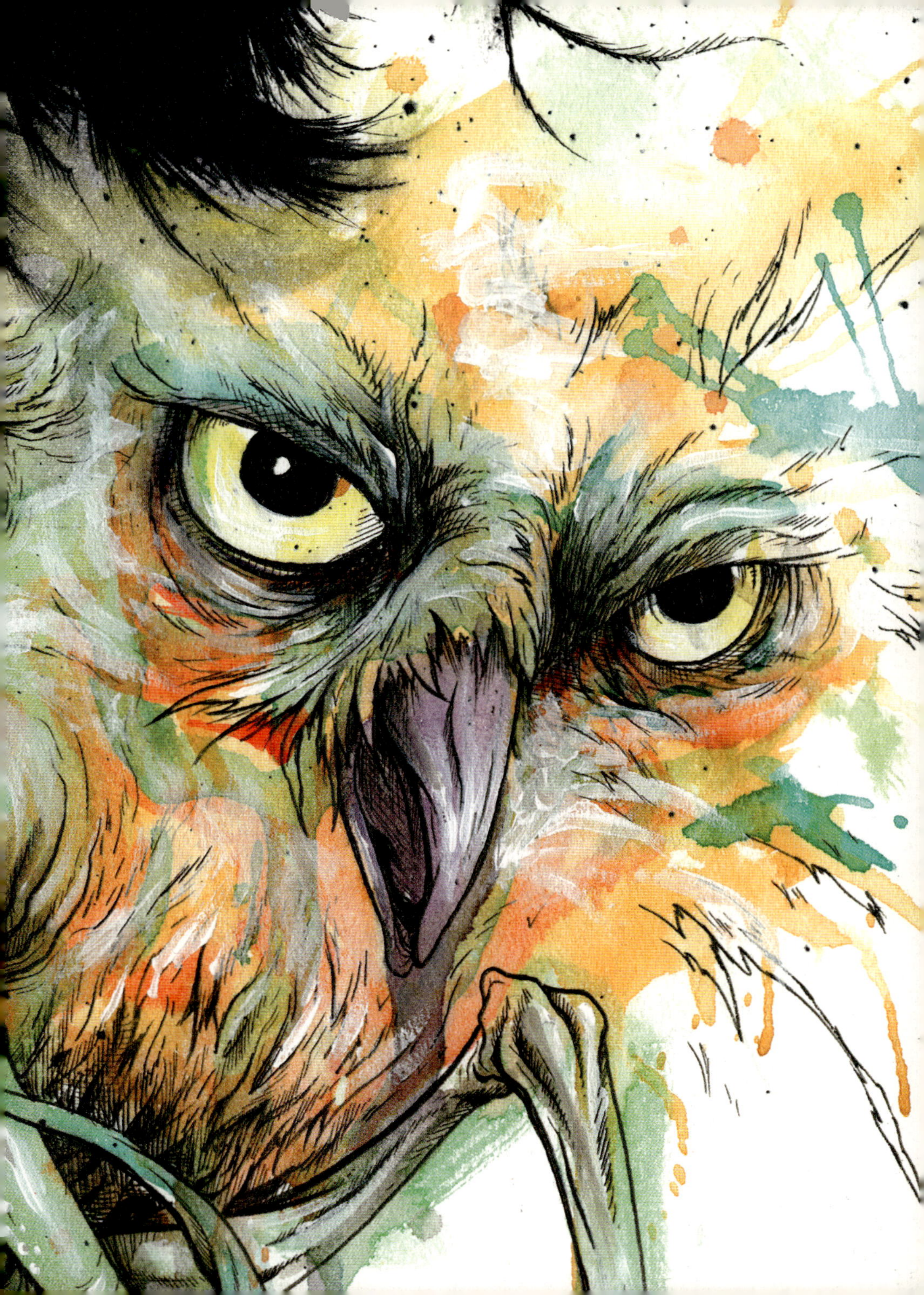

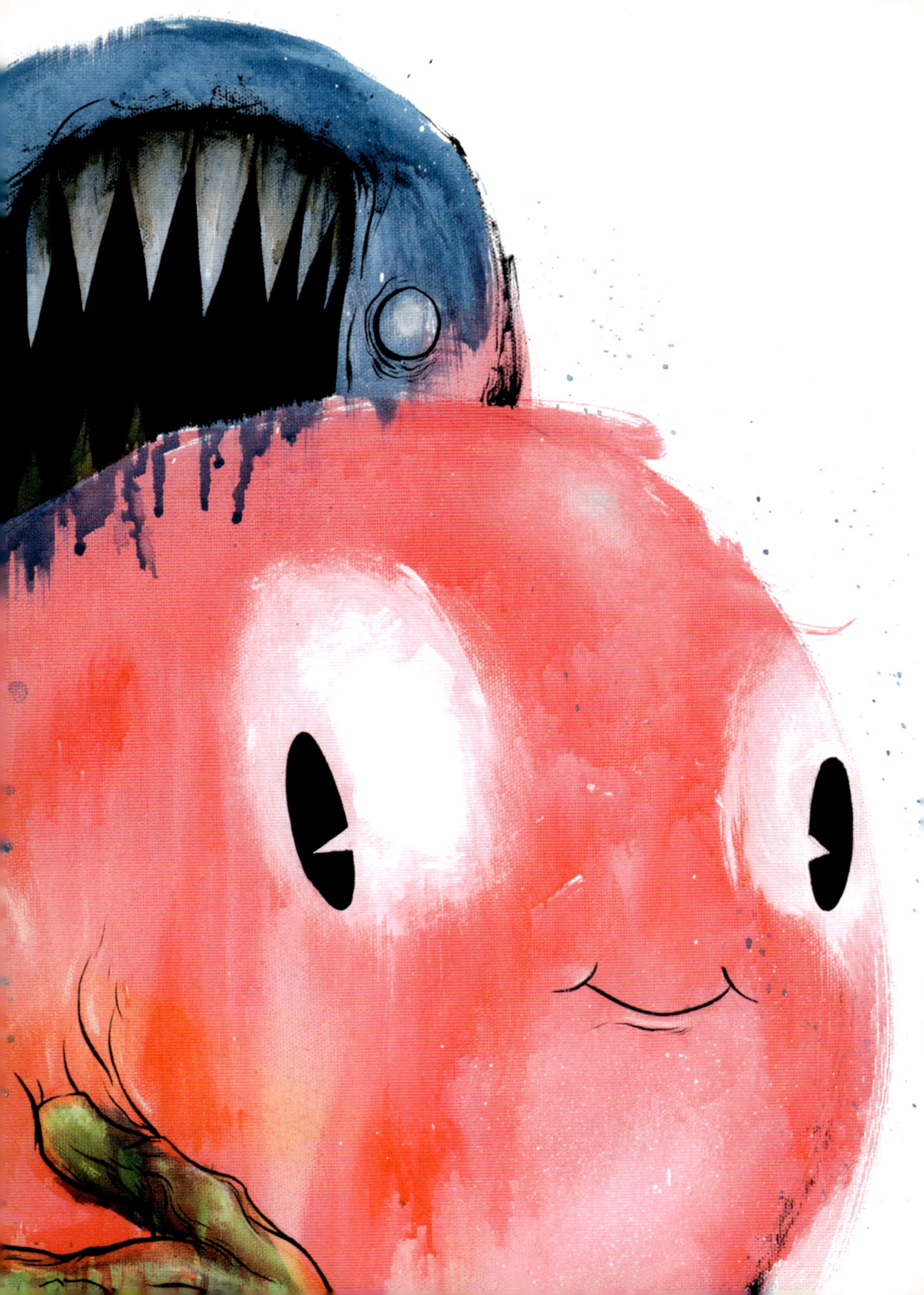

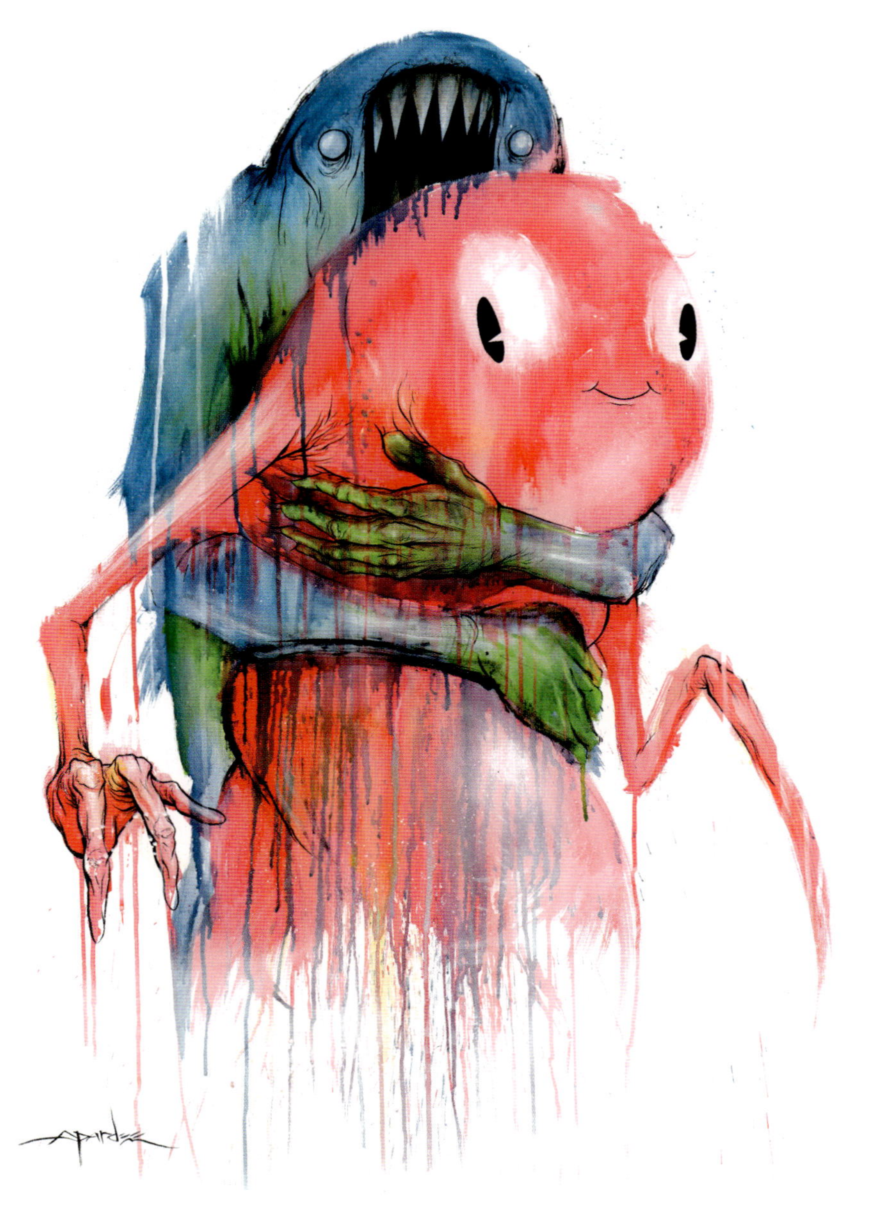

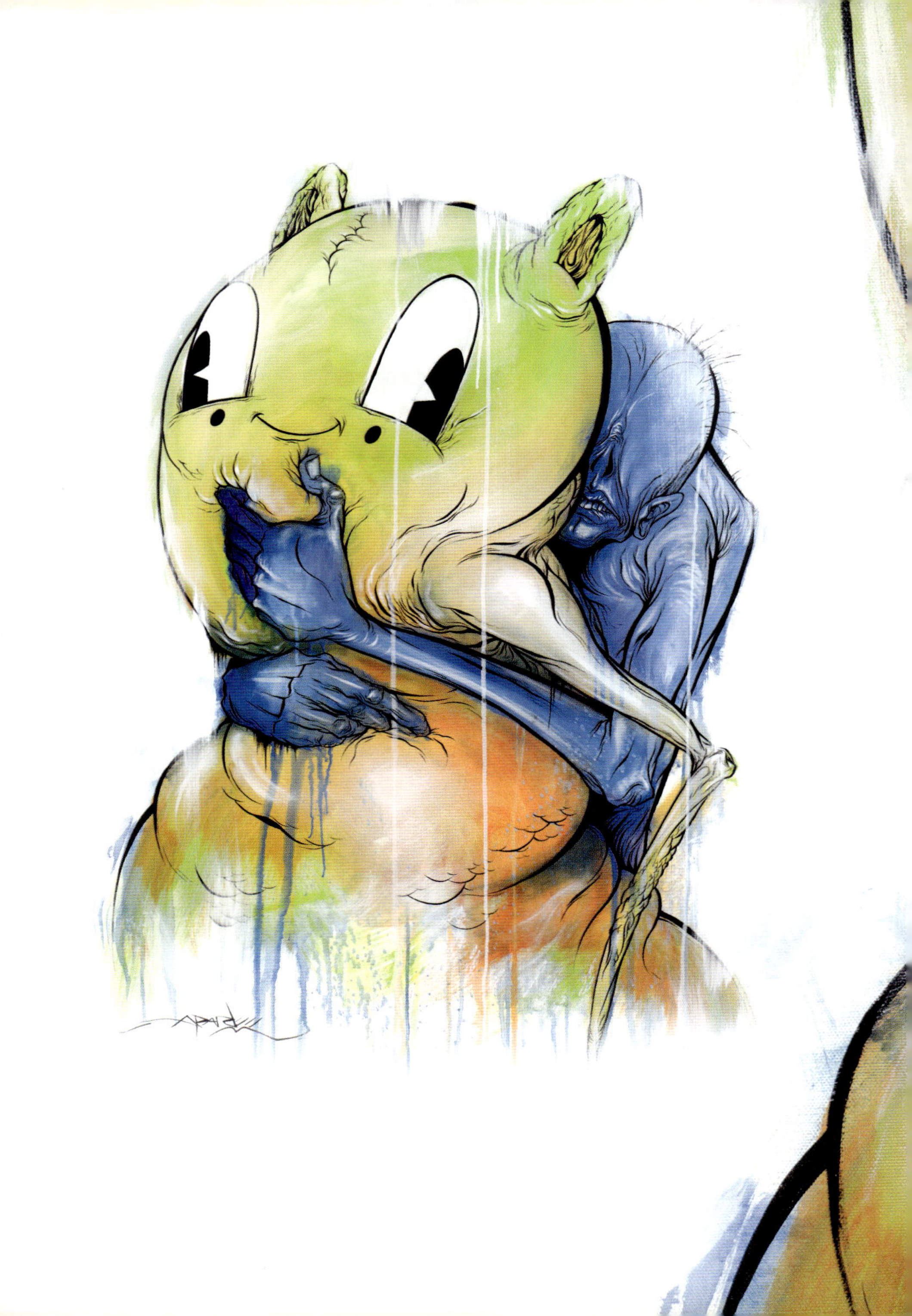

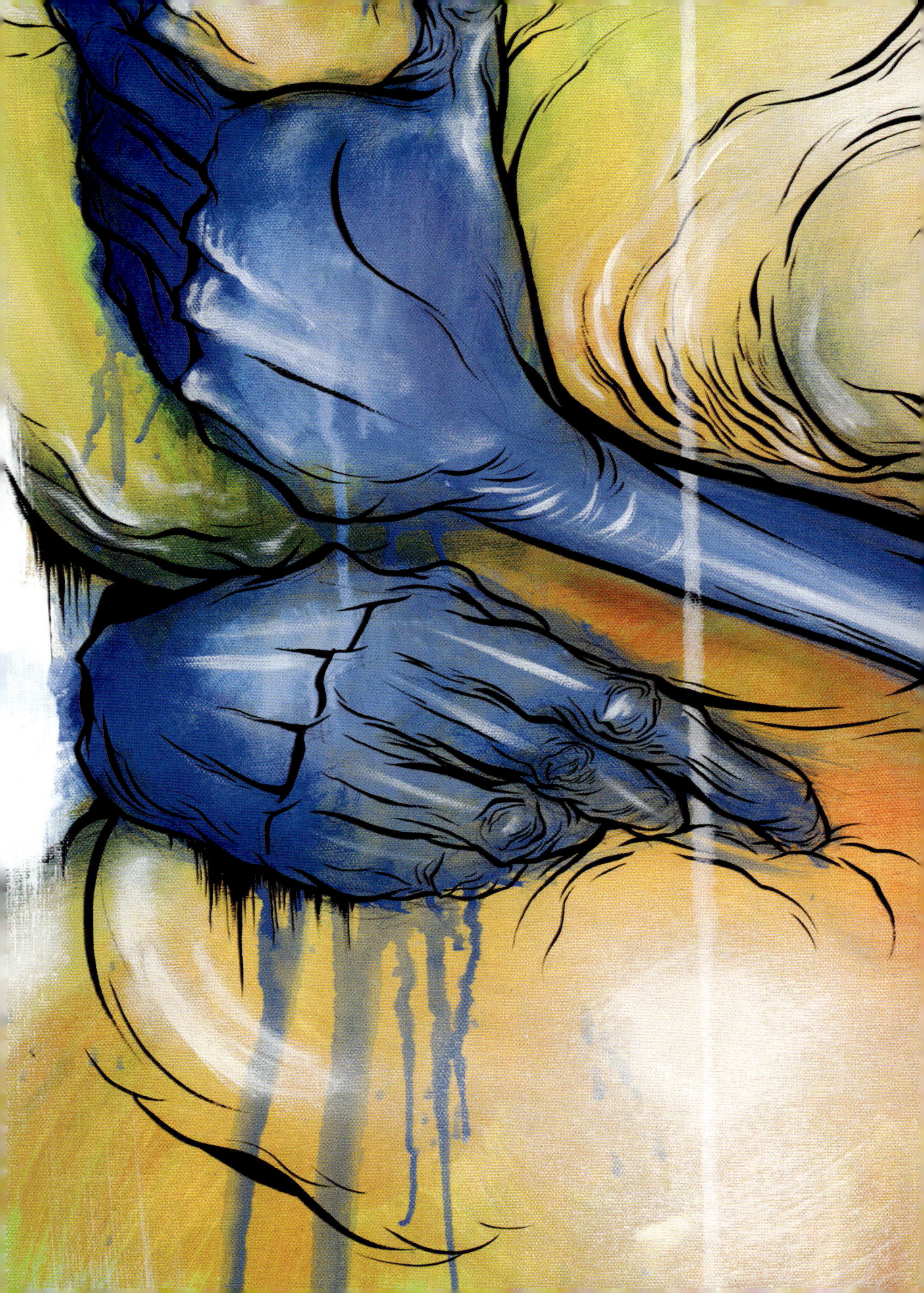

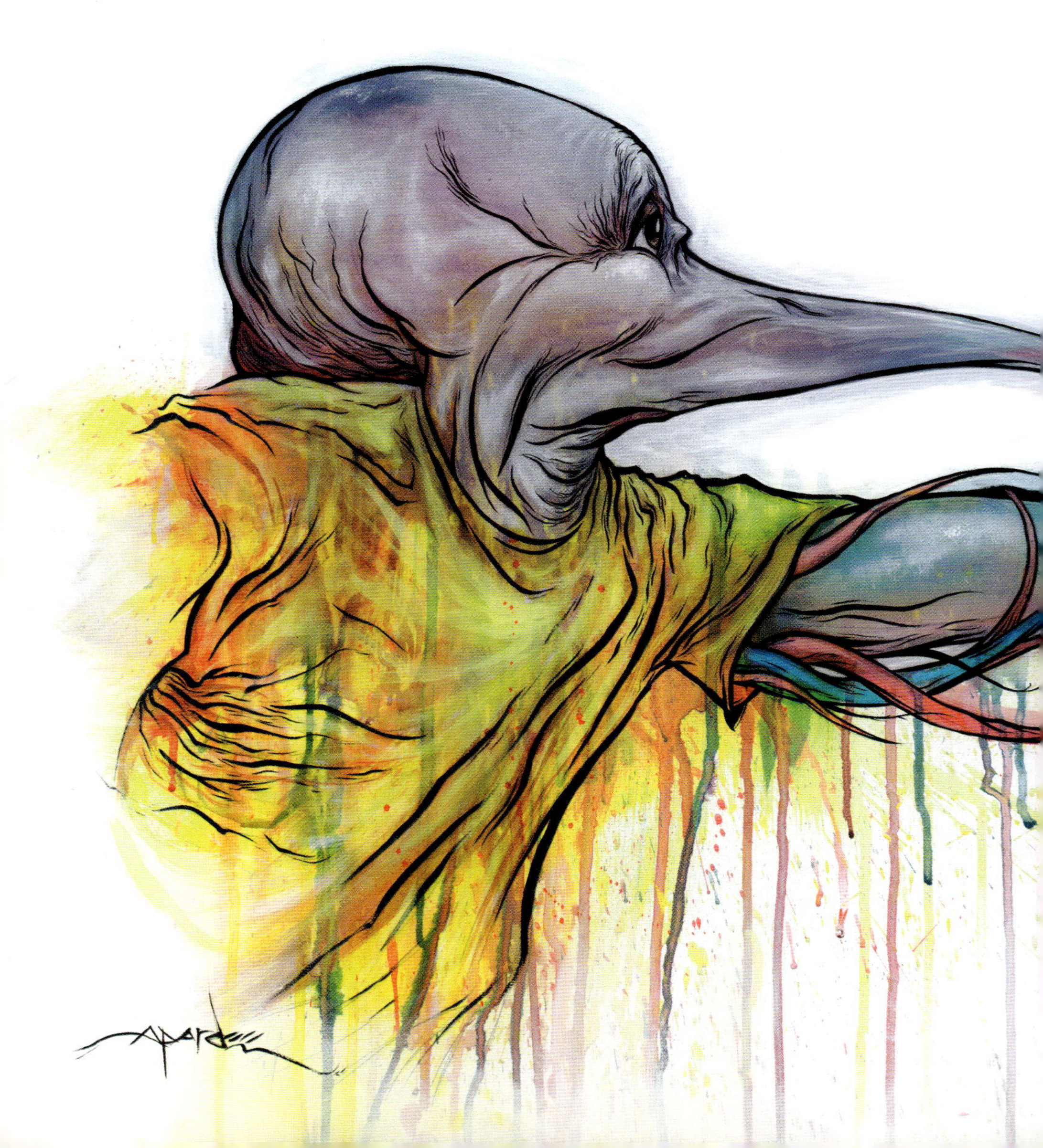

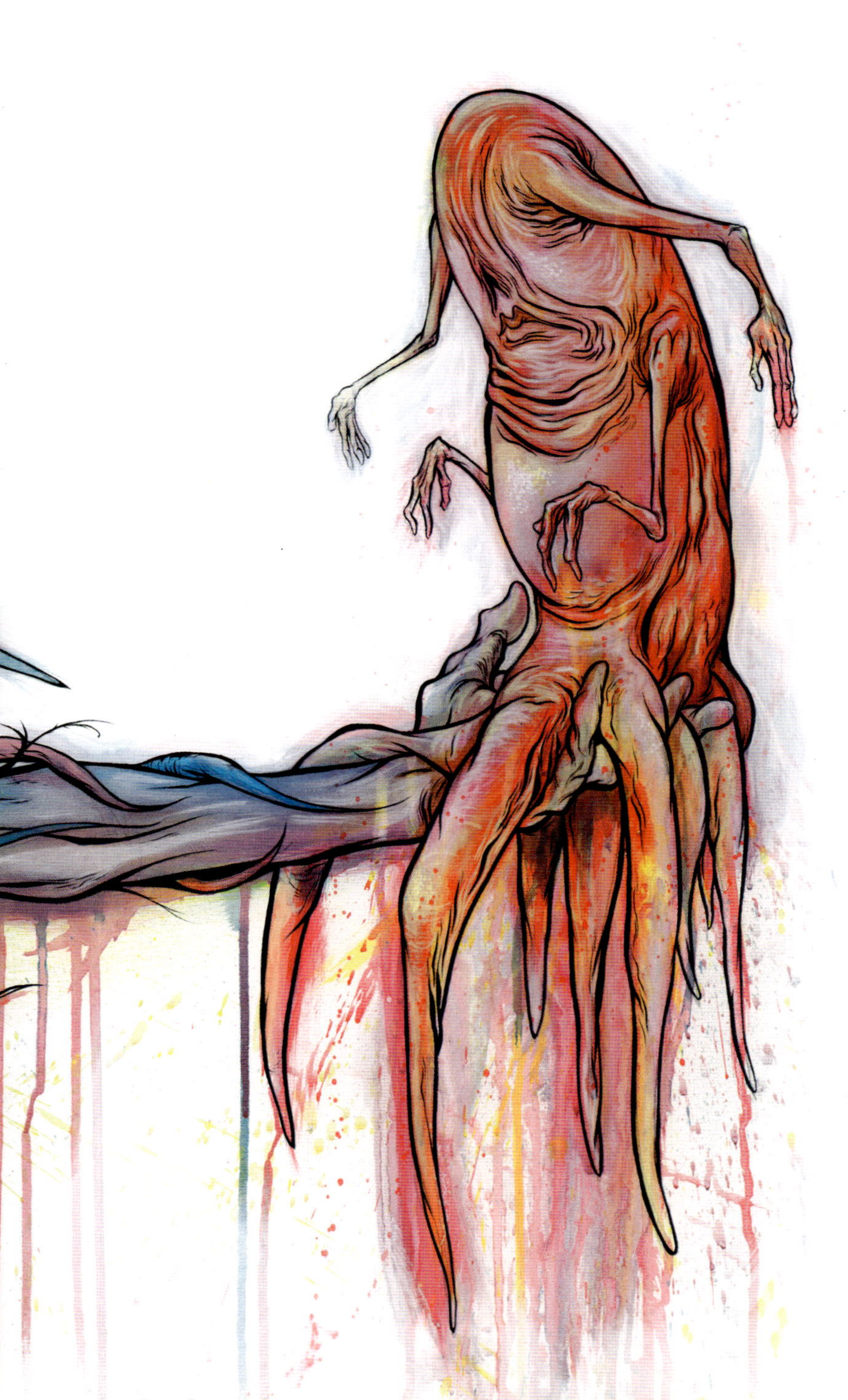

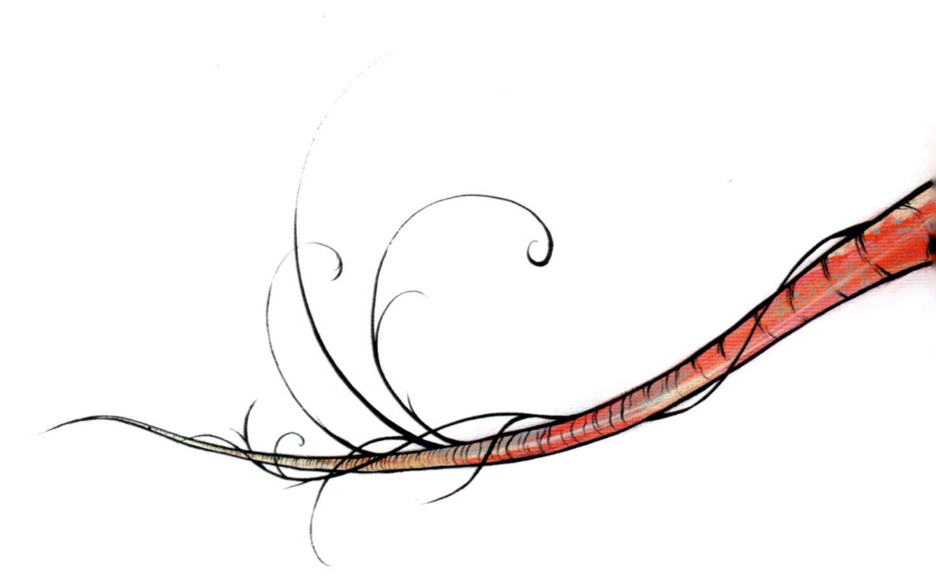

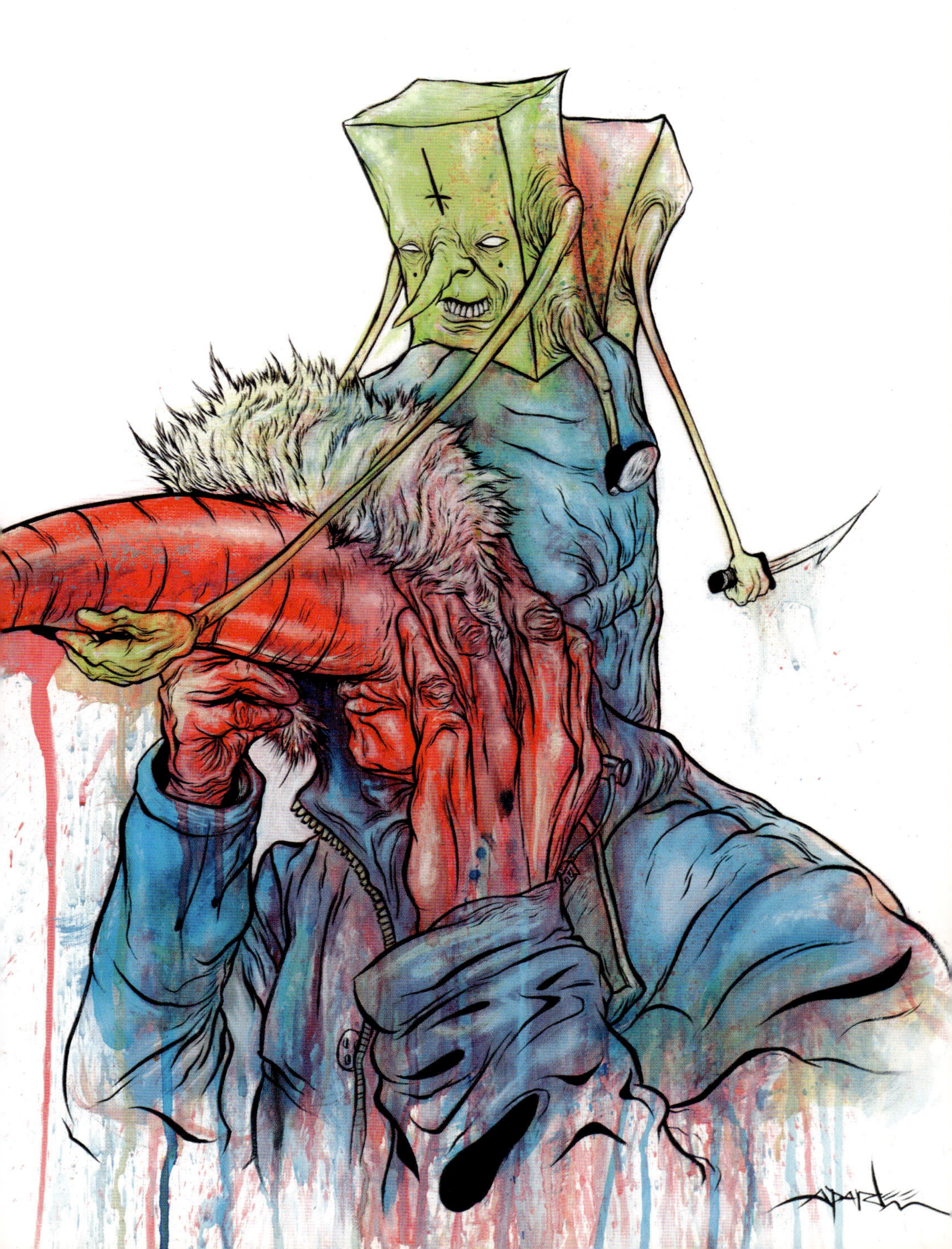

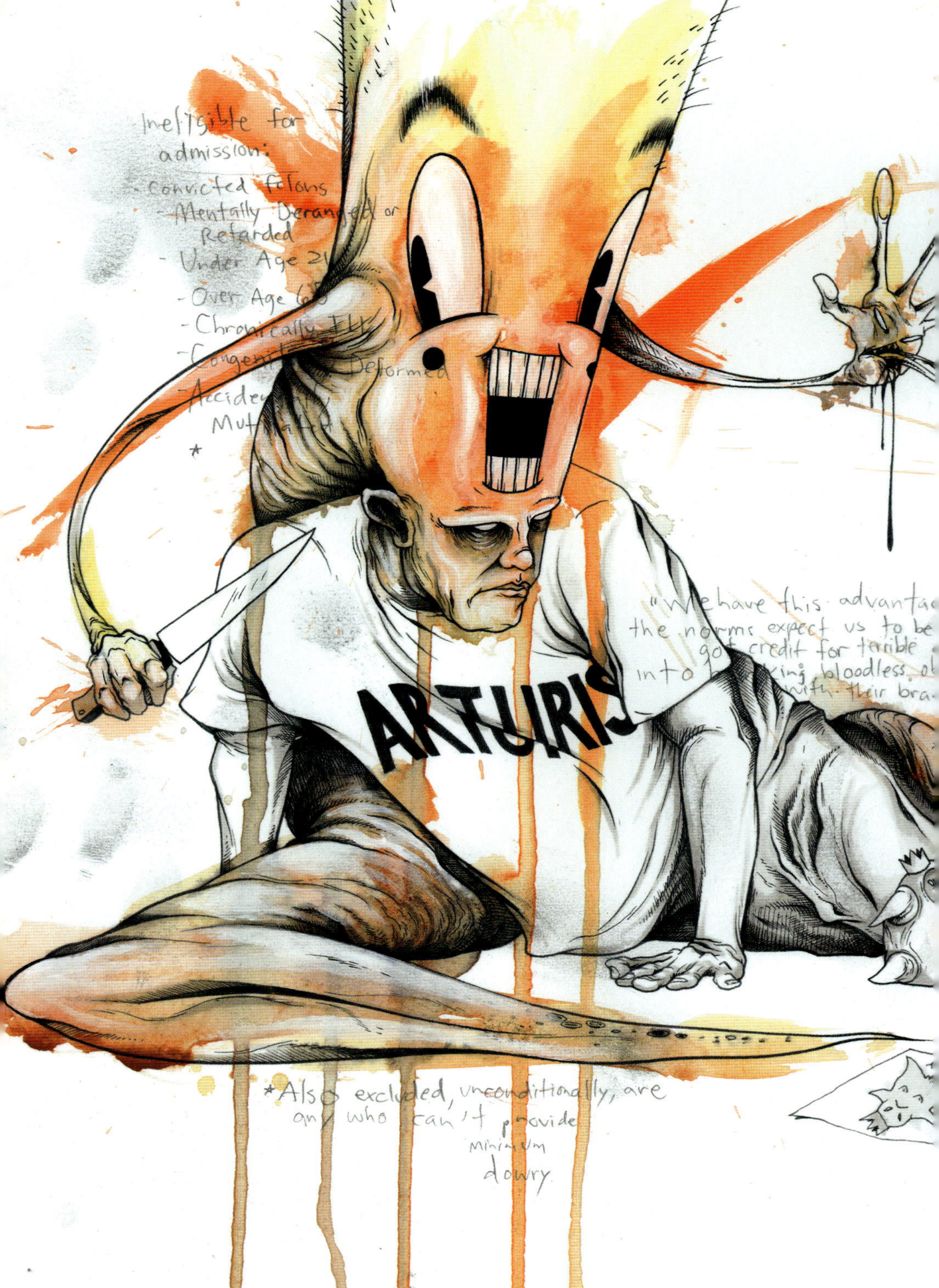

Ineligible for
admission:
- Convicted felons
- Mentally Deranged or
Retarded
- Under Age 21
- Over Age
- Chronically Ill
- Congenit
Deformed
- Accide
Mut
*
"We have this advanta
the norms expect us to be
got credit for terrible
into
bloodless
with their bra
ARTURIS
*Also excluded, unconditionally, are
any who can't provide
minimum
dowry

ven a rats-ass dwarf jester
isguised in his foolery. Freaks are like owls, mythed
The Norms figure our contact
e is shaky. They see us
t off from
mptation
and
pettiness.
ven our
hate is
grand
by
their
lights.
And
the more
deformed
we
are,
the
higher
our supposed sanctity."

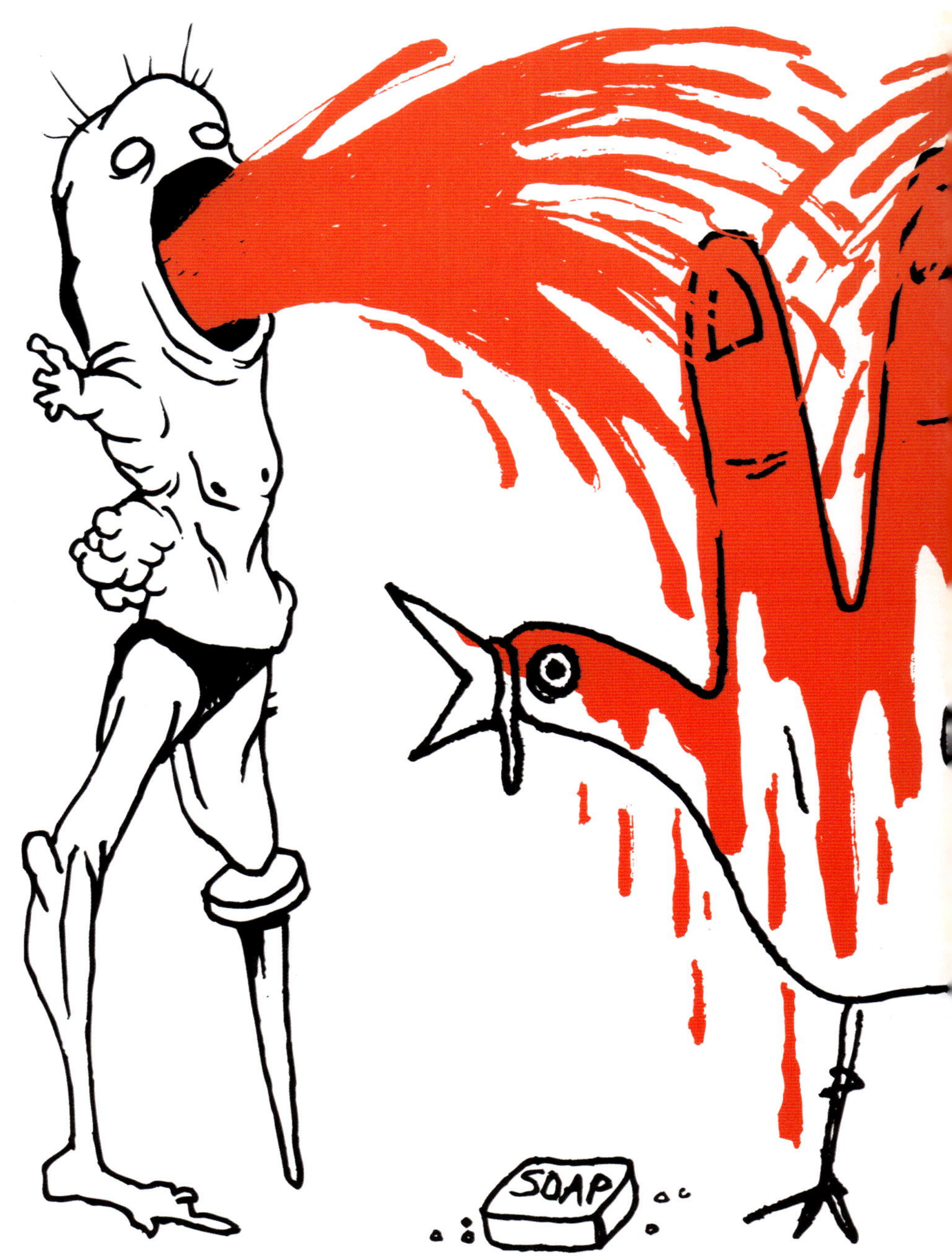
SOAP

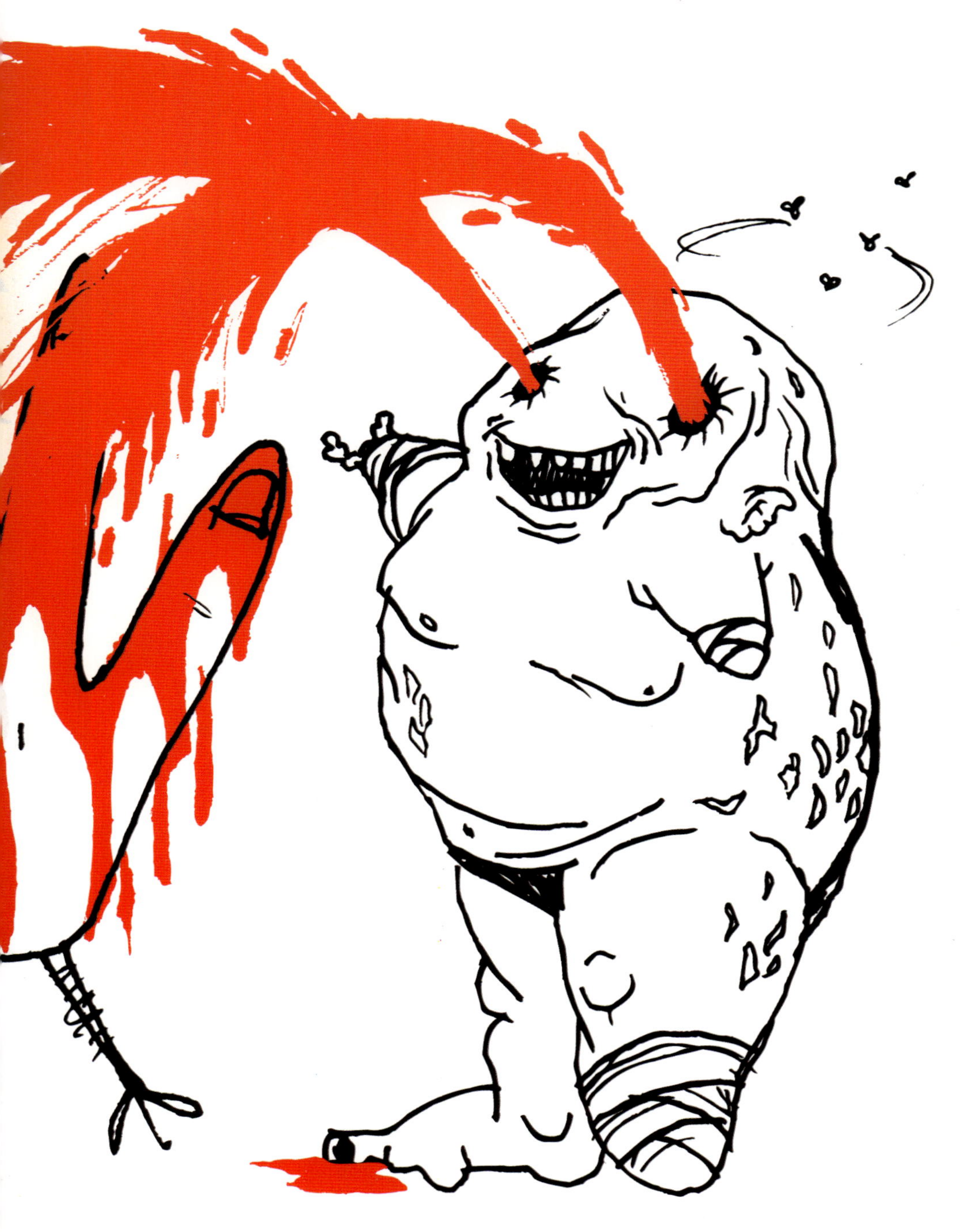

I COULDN'T HAVE MADE THIS WITHOUT THE FOLLOWING PEOPLE WHO, RIGHT NOW, I REALLY LIKE:

MATT REVELLI AND EVERYONE AT UPPER PLAYGROUND, ANYA LEEDS, MY FAMILY, ZEROFRIENDS, MAYBE THAT MONSTER IN CLOVERFIELD BUT I'M NOT SURE BECAUSE THAT MOVIE DOESN'T START FOR 3 DAYS SO I MAY REGRET THAT, QUAKE, PASTIME, JEBEN BERG ROBERT BOWEN, PAUL BUSTAMANTE, CRAOLA, JON WAYSHAK, STEVE REEDY, DAVE CORREIA, SEAN PIERCE, TOPR, CAGE AND THE WEATHERMEN, THE USED, LORDS, CBS, UM, CARDBOARD CITY, AND THE GURPNESS.

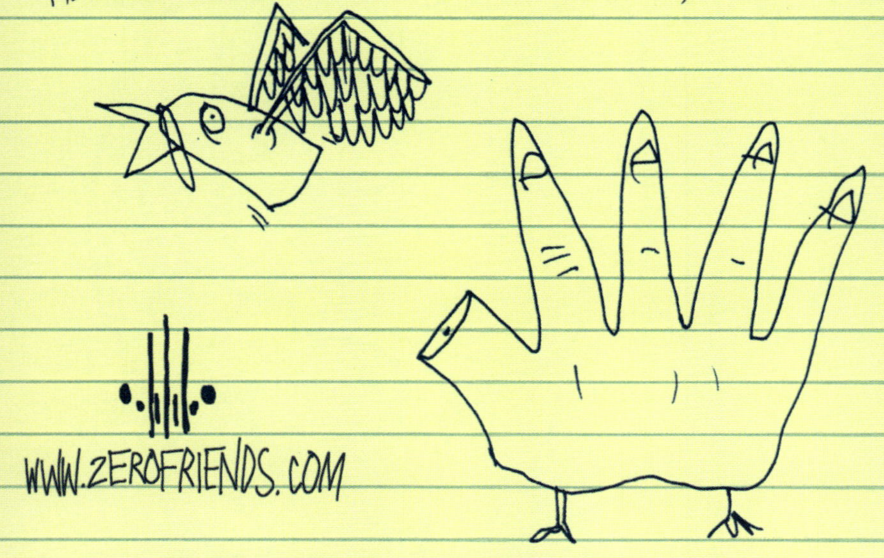

~~P.S. MY DAD WAS A LIBRARIAN FOR YEARS~~

P.S. DAD, YOU WERE A LIBRARIAN FOR YEARS SO HOPEFULLY YOU WILL APPRECIATE THE FACT THAT I FINALLY MADE A BOOK WITH A HARD COVER, EVEN IF THERE'S NOT REALLY ANY WORDS IN IT. LOVE,

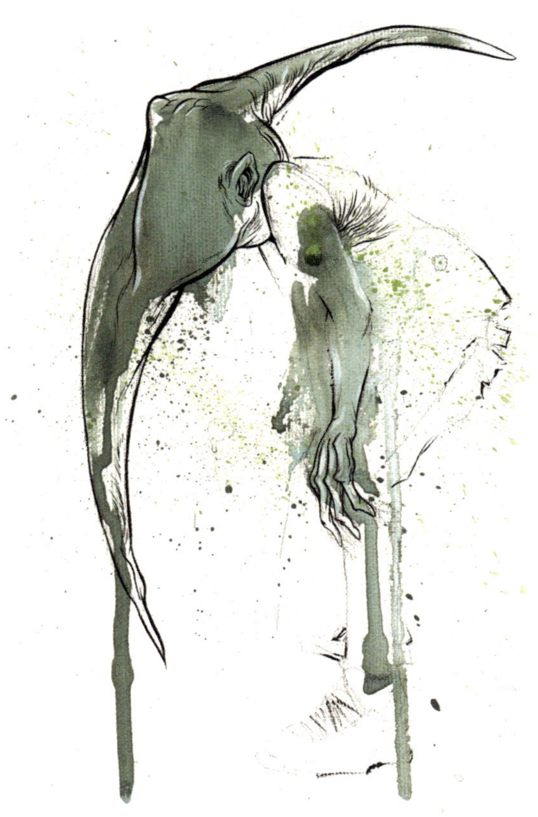

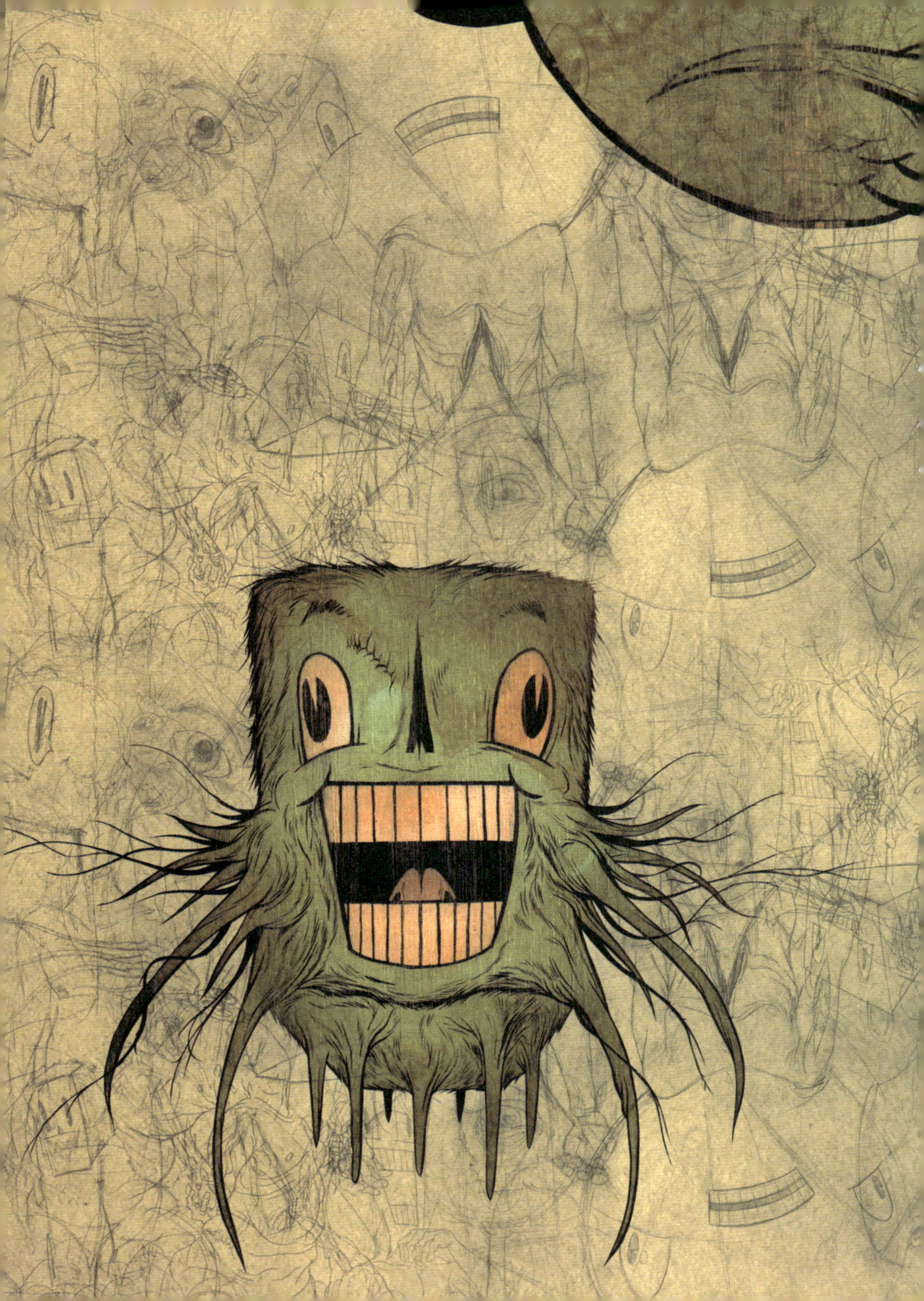